His Princess™ Retreat
WORKBOOK

P9-DUB-364

This Workbook Belongs To:

_____

WORKBOOK

His Princess™
Retreat
Weekend

Sheri Rose SHEPHERD

www.hisprincess.com
602-407-8789

Published by
Treasure Publishing
P.O. Box 68807
Portland, OR 97268
503-656-9443
978-1-934384-10-7
Printed in Canada

Cover design and inside pages
John Lewis

Sheri Rose
SHEPHERD

Sheri Rose is a woman who can relate to almost any woman's battle. This Best-Selling Author and Motivational Speaker grew up in a dysfunctional home and was severely overweight as a teen. As a young woman, she battled with depression and a severe eating disorder. She understands the pain that comes from a broken home and she knows what it means to fight for freedom from your past... In spite of an English teacher telling her she was "born to lose" and a learning disorder - dyslexia - Sheri Rose has (in God's strength) written many best-selling books, founded His Princess Ministries and speaks to thousands each year at churches and women's conferences. She was most recently named #1 show of the year on Focus on the Family broadcast.

Introduction by Sheri Rose

Princesses Are Not Perfect...The Pressure Is Off

Even if godly people fall down seven times, they always get up.
Proverbs 24:16 NIRV

I know how hard it is to think of ourselves as royalty. Each of us know our weaknesses and imperfections all too well! So let me take the pressure off you: No man or woman in the Bible or in Christian history, nor any believer who did something great to further God's Kingdom, lived a perfect life. Our God can and will take whatever we have experienced or done; good or bad and use it for His glory. He is waiting to turn our failures, our difficult circumstances, our pain and whatever this life brings into something significant that will further His Kingdom. My prayer for you as we go through this study together is that you will begin to believe you are who God says you are and that your Daddy in Heaven will do for you and through you all that is promised in His Word.

HIS PRINCESS LOVE LETTER TO YOU

My Princess,

I chose you before the foundation of the earth to be my princess. You are royalty even though at times you don't feel like a princess. I will wait for you until you are ready to start living out the amazing plans that I have for you. I know that you don't know where to begin or how to live as the princess I've called you to be, so let me teach you day by day. Start by recognizing who I am: King of kings, Lord of lords, and the Lover of your soul. When the two of us begin to meet alone together every day, I will show you how to live as My chosen princess. But remember, my child, just as I have chosen you, I have given you a choice about whether or not to represent Me to the world. If you are willing, I am here to give you all you need to fulfill that royal calling.

Love,
Your King who has chosen you.

> *"Out of all the peoples on the face of the earth, the Lord
> has chosen you to be His treasured possession"*
> Deuteronomy 14:2, NIV

Don't you love knowing that we don't have to earn our
Father's love and approval? Our King loves us no
matter how many times we fall. He is always there
to pick us up, heal our hearts, and help us finish this
race of our faith.

Write a prayer of thanks to your Father, the King of
all kings, for choosing you to be His Princess…

_____

_____

_____

_____

_____

_____

_____

_____

_____

_____

_____

What an honor to be God's princesses—and we didn't have to compete for the crown. Our King has chosen us, and we didn't need to do anything to win His attention, His favor, or His love. My Sister Princess, you have already won His heart, and He has gifted you personally to do something great for His kingdom!

HIS PRINCESS DEVOTION

Take Your Royal Position

*For you are a chosen people. You are royal priests, a holy
nation, God's very own possession. As a result, you can
show others the goodness of God, for he called you out of
the darkness into his wonderful light.*
1 Peter 2:9, NLT

As I waited for the big announcement, I began to think,
Is this really what I need and want—to win a worldly
crown? As the envelope that held the winner's name
was passed to the master of ceremonies, I glanced at
the panel of judges. Am I placing my sense of worth
in the hands of these people's evaluation of me? Then
my eyes moved to the other women competing for the
same crown. Each of them must have a story to tell
and something to share with the world if she should be
crowned. Somehow it did not seem right that only one
of us would be chosen.

The countdown began with the fourth runner-up. My
stomach was in knots as the master of ceremonies slowly announced the judges' decisions. Each of us left standing on stage after a runner-up was named felt a trembling

hope of winning and an impossible-to-ignore fear of rejection.

Then the master of ceremonies called my name as the 1994 Mrs. United States of America. Overwhelmed with joy, I cried as that worldly crown was placed on my head and the crystal-beaded banner was hung over my shoulder. Cameras flashed, people applauded, and women gathered around me to celebrate my victory. It was one of those moments in life that I will never forget.

However, when the cameras stopped flashing, the audience emptied out of the auditorium, the celebration came to an end, and I walked back to my hotel room. I took off the crown and laid it on the table by the window. I turned off the lights and noticed that the crystal crown sparkled with the reflection of the full moon and the bright Las Vegas lights.

As I stared at the beautiful crown that I had so longed for, I began to think about my Lord. I remembered the night when, in my darkest hour, He had crowned me with His tender love and mercy. It had happened ten years earlier in a different hotel room. Before I knew the King, I felt hopeless and desperate for someone or something to fill my empty soul.

Back then, I had all the things that should have meant happiness and fulfillment. I was no longer abusing drugs, I had lost sixty pounds, and I owned my own business. I had money, success, beauty titles, boyfriends, nice clothes, and people's approval for all I had overcome. I drove a nice car and had a calendar full of appointments of places to go and people to see. Yet I still cried myself to sleep at night and battled depression as well as an eating disorder called bulimia. On the outside I looked like I had it all together, but on the inside I was falling apart. I felt empty and alone even when I was in a crowd of people. I could not find anything or anyone to fill that deep lonely place in my heart. I wanted to die and I could not break free from bulimia or deep depression.

- **Weight loss could only change my body...**
  it could not change my life.

- **Money could only buy me things...**
  But it could not buy me peace of mind or a home in Heaven.

- **Success could win me people's praises...
  but it could not give me a purpose for living**

Feeling as if I had nothing more to live for and deciding that I could not go on any longer, I checked into a hotel room. My plan was to end my life with an overdose of sleeping pills. Yet, at that moment as I entered the room to end my life, I felt led to cry out to God out of desperation. At that moment in the hotel room, I actually felt God's holy presence with me. He heard my cry and rescued me before I took my life. For the first time in my life I did not feel alone. I felt loved and at peace.

If Jesus is your Savior, then you have been appointed as a Daughter of the King of kings. *You have an amazing crown...the crown of everlasting life.* You wear the most important banner of all...the banner of His name. You have power inside of you—the King's very Spirit—to do great things that will echo throughout all eternity.

Session One

HIS PRINCESS IN ACTION

Royal Reflection

A worldly princess… glorifies herself
His Princess… glorifies her King

A worldly princess… cares about her needs and desires
His Princess… is more concerned about the needs of others

A worldly princess… will be known for her comfort
His Princess… will be known for her character and courage

A worldly princess… invests her time and talent in the here and now
His Princess …invests her time and talent in eternity

A worldly princess' reign… will end
His Princess' reign …. Will Last Forever!!!

Anyone can choose to be a worldly princess...But you my Sister Princess have been handpicked by the King to be His Princess!

You must choose to take your God-given appointed position. While you are here you can choose to hide out in caves of comfort and miss the crowning moment to make a difference, or choose to let your life leave a legacy.

Write a prayer to your King and ask Him to open your eyes that you might see who you really are....His chosen Daughter.

_____

_____

_____

_____

_____

_____

_____

_____

_____

_____

GROUP DISCUSSION
Freedom for His Princess

1. Read the Scriptures below to the group.

Wherever the Spirit of the Lord is, there is freedom
2 Corinthians 3:17, NLT

*How joyful are those who fear the LORD and delight
in obeying his commands. Their children will be
successful everywhere; an entire generation of godly
people will be blessed. They themselves will be
wealthy, and their good deeds will last forever.*
Psalm 112:1-3, NIV

2. Have each person answer below…
What Has God revealed to you about true freedom through this message?

_____

_____

_____

_____

_____

_____

3. Read 1 Peter 4:10 out loud to the group.

*God has given each of you a gift from his great variety
of spiritual gifts. Use them well to serve one another.*
1 Peter 4:10, NLT

4. Have each person answer below...
What gift has God placed inside of you and what
do feel is your appointed position?

_____

_____

_____

_____

_____

_____

_____

_____

_____

_____

_____

_____

_____

_____

5. Read this His Princess Love Letter out loud to the group.

Dear Princess,

I long for you to know freedom from guilt and anger, from fear and worry, from hopelessness and purposelessness. I loved you with My life so that you can be free of such things. Nothing in this world—nothing except you yourself, My love, can keep you from walking in My freedom. So come to Me and read My Word. Cry out to Me, My love, and I will give you the keys to living in freedom. You will become my princess warrior when you pray and obey My voice. I will never hurt you or leave you alone, so come to Me, My daughter, and I, your Daddy in Heaven, will soothe your soul, restore your peace of mind, and set your precious feet on solid ground.

Love,
Your King and your Freedom.

6. Close in Prayer.

7. Have everyone do their personal study during the week.

HIS PRINCESS PERSONAL STUDY TIME

Freedom

*M*any of us know the Lord personally but….feel anything but free!

Our King sent His only son to die for our freedom. Our Prince loves us so passionately that He gave His life so that we may live in total freedom from guilt, anger, and pain rooted in our past; from the problems in our present; and from fear of our future. Jesus paid too great a price on that cross for us to live defeated, powerless lives! Praise God for His Word and its winning plan for living a victorious life—victorious over the world, the flesh, and the devil; victorious over sin; victorious over darkness and hopelessness.

The Word of the Lord (the Bible) is filled with true stories about real battles against God's people. And, in every battle our King gives a plan for victory. However, He also gives His people a choice to win His way or to be defeated by fighting their way. This teaching is about winning the war against the enemy of our soul and living in the victory Jesus has already won. It's time to win the greatest battle of all …the battle in our mind and emotions. I pray as we study His plan for our freedom that you will choose life…His way.

For the LORD your God is going with you!
He will fight for you against your enemies, and he
will give you victory!
Deuteronomy 20:4, NLT

HIS PRINCESS DEVOTION

One of the deceiver's favorite tricks is to make us feel that all is hopeless, but the truth is that the Lord will give us victory!

Remember the Israelites? God rescued them and brought them out of slavery in Egypt—and immediately to the edge of the Red Sea. There the chosen, rescued people stood, stuck between what looked like a sea of hopelessness and their enemies charging toward them. I am sure they felt abandoned and defeated, and we know they questioned why God had set them free if they were going to die defeated by their Egyptian enemies. However, it was that hopeless situation that God used to destroy their Egyptian enemies once and for all! And that sea of hopelessness gave God another opportunity to prove His power: He parted the waters and His people walked on dry land to their freedom. Then He closed the waters, and the Israelites watched their enemies die before their very eyes. Many times life's greatest trials give us greater faith. The Israelites did not have to do anything to see victory except walk to their freedom through the open door their God provided.

God wants to carry you into victory my Sister Princess! He has an open door for you. I know that your circumstances may seem hopeless; but, God has great things in store for you if you will walk in faith. Let's journey together into the seven steps of F.R.E.E.D.O.M.

A PRINCESS PRAYER OVER YOU

Dear Lord,

I ask today that You would open my sister's eyes and heart to the Freedom You hold for her. Let her see that it is a gift, a special treasure, that she will receive as she learns to let go of worry, guilt, shame, and whatever keeps her from fully experiencing You, Lord God. We claim victory in the name of Jesus today Lord! Lead her and deliver her through her sea of hopelessness. Prove Your power through her as she commits these next days to You Lord, and lead her to complete Freedom!

In Jesus' name I pray, amen.

The Plan for His Princess

F.R.E.E.D.O.M.

People often ask me "How did you break free from…your past, your poor choices, your eating disorder, and your depression?"

My answer is…

Wherever the Spirit of the Lord is there is freedom.
2 Corinthians 3:1, NLT

HIS PRINCESS DEVOTION

King Solomon had it all; wealth, women and power. Yet, in the book of Ecclesiastes he describes life as meaningless. There was only one thing that King Solomon did not have…a battle to fight. However, His father King David fought many battles in his lifetime. He fought a battle against a giant in the land that was coming against God's people. His courage and faith birthed his public ministry and made him a spiritual hero. David fought a battle against countless enemies which carved character and prepared him for the royal call God had on his life. He battled with insecurity so he waited in a cave for his calling. However, that battle helped him find his confidence in God alone. He was also in a battle for his very life while Saul was trying to have him killed. His battle with fear for his life birthed real faith in the future king. And in his pain he wrote many of the Psalms we read today in the Bible. He had a battle with his father who did not even consider David as the son who could have been chosen by God to become the future king. The interesting thing to me is that the one time David was not fighting a battle he fell into sin with Bathsheba and had her husband killed to cover his sin. Many times our battles in this life prepare us for our purpose.

So the goal in our walk with God should not be to dodge the pain and problems this life brings, but to learn to fight the good fight and finish strong! Wouldn't it be great to be able to say at the end of our days on this earth as Paul did…

> *I have fought a good fight, I have finished the race, and I have remained faithful. And now the prize awaits me—the crown of righteousness that the Lord, the righteous Judge, will give me on that great day of his return. And the prize is not just for me but for all who eagerly look forward to his glorious return.*
> 2 Timothy 4:7–8, NLT

F.R.E.E.D.O.M.

Find the root of the pain or problem...

For you are a slave to whatever controls you.
2 Peter 2:1, NLT

If we don't find out what's causing us pain or problems, then it will end up controlling us. Pretending that our pain isn't real won't make it go away. In fact, if we continue to ignore our hurts, no matter how long ago or how recently they happened, they will eventually defeat us. I know from experience how hard it is to get real, but the only way to complete healing is the path of truth! Remember God's promise, "Those who sow with tears will reap with joy." (Psalm 126:5, NKJV) People ask me again and again after I speak about my life, "How did you get past the pain?" My answer is, "Every time it hurt, I cried out to my Daddy in Heaven, and every tear began cleansing my soul."

HIS PRINCESS DEVOTION

*I*f you don't find the root, the root will find you!

I also know how hard it is to find the time to heal. The list of demands on us as wives and mothers, as homemakers and cooks, as tutors and chauffeurs, as personal shoppers and school volunteers can seem endless. These demands wear us out, and our exhaustion affects us emotionally. We find ourselves discouraged and depressed. And putting more pressure on us, some well-meaning Christians have said that we need to ignore our feelings and live by faith. My question to them is this: If we are supposed to ignore our feelings, then why did God give them to us in the first place?

God created us in His image. He has feelings, and we do too. Did you know that the Bible refers to God's emotions more than two thousand times?

Ephesians 4:26 says, "Be angry, and yet do not sin" (NASB). It is not a sin to feel angry, hurt, overwhelmed, or out of control. It is how we respond that becomes a sin when we allow these feelings to effect our actions and do not deal with the root of why we have the emotions in the first place. The way to deal with our feelings—the only way to get out from under their control over us—is to find out what is causing them. Unfortunately, many of us have hidden hurts so deeply in our hearts that we don't feel anything at all anymore. We have become "Barbies' with a Bible." We look like all is well on the outside but feel empty on the inside. So when life hits, our heart aches and we struggle to identify what is causing our actions or reactions. If that's the case, it's time to fall on our faces and cry out to the all-knowing, living God that truly loves us and wants to heal us—the One who knows everything that's hidden in our hearts no matter how good of an actress we are.

O LORD, you have searched me and you know me.
You know when I sit and when I rise; you perceive my
thoughts from afar. You discern my going out and my
lying down; you are familiar with all my ways.
Psalm 139:1-3, NIV

Take a moment to find out what is really controlling you by taking the test below

Issue	Often	Sometimes	Rarely
Exhausted	☐	☐	☐
Depressed	☐	☐	☐
Over Eating	☐	☐	☐
Control Issues	☐	☐	☐
Excessively Busy	☐	☐	☐
Anger	☐	☐	☐
Anxiety	☐	☐	☐
Self-Destructive	☐	☐	☐
Obsessive/Compulsive	☐	☐	☐
Unhealthy Relationships	☐	☐	☐
Fearful	☐	☐	☐
Poor Health	☐	☐	☐
Needing Approval	☐	☐	☐
Emotionally out of control	☐	☐	☐

HIS PRINCESS PRAYER

Dear Jesus,

I feel (fill in what you feel) _____, and I don't want to live in this emotional place any longer. As frightening as this is for me right now, I pray, Father God, that You would reveal the root of my unhealthy actions and reactions. I need You to show me what is going on inside of me so that I can give my heart and all of its hurts to You. I want to change, and I ask you to intervene now and show me what I need to do to be healed and be whole. I am ready to let you remove the root of my pain. Thank you for being my safe place, and thank you that I can come to You with anything. I love You and I praise You for Your faithfulness to me. Now, by the work of Your Holy Spirit, please help me.

In Your name I pray, amen.

HIS PRINCESS IN ACTION

*B*e still and listen as God helps you recognize the root of your feelings. Then write down what He reveals. Writing it down makes it become real and gives you a touchstone for taking the next step toward freedom.

> *"Then you will know the truth,*
> *and the truth will set you free."*
> John 8:32, NIV

_____

_____

_____

_____

_____

_____

_____

_____

_____

_____

_____

_____

_____

_____

_____

F.**R**.E.E.D.O.M.

Run to God

Once you discover the root of your feelings, you may hurt even more than when you were hiding those feelings. Know that in order to truly be healed, you have to feel that pain. In your pain, cry out to your King until He wipes away every tear. I promise He will.

HIS PRINCESS DEVOTION

*K*ing David cried out to God every time he was hurting, and he is known as "a man after God's own heart." There was nothing artificial about David's relationship with the Lord. He didn't hide his rage, his fears, his disappointments, his worries, his praise, or his love from his heavenly Father. If you have not experienced that same closeness with your Lord, it may be because you have never known how to let yourself be entirely honest with Him.

Don't listen when the enemy whispers that you can save yourself from the pain and problems of this world. When something hurts you or someone angers you, tell your Savior! He died a very real death for you to have access to the throne room of God. He is our place of rest, our safe place. When we are in His presence, He will restore our mind, our body, and our soul.

Our Father in Heaven wants His Daughter to be free! No one loves you more, and no one else has the power or passion for you that your God has. He alone is the only one who can and will heal your heart and soothe your soul. He is the Lover of your soul, and He longs for you to run to Him so that He can heal your every hurt. If you truly want to be a woman after God's own heart, and want to experience the complete healing God offers you, then run to Him every time you hurt. He is your Daddy in Heaven, and He longs to comfort and heal you.

HIS PRINCESS LOVE LETTER TO YOU

*M*y Princess, it's okay to cry,

I see how hard you try to handle your heart and I know you want to live a life without heartache or pain, My love. But I am asking you to take a step closer to Me, your Daddy in Heaven that loves and adores you, by crying out to me rather than trying to be strong in your own strength. I am not expecting you to pretend pain is not real. The truth is your tears will wash your soul from the inside out. I will heal your broken heart if you will trust Me with all the pieces. I am your deliverer My Daughter, and key to true freedom. So cry out to Me. Feel Me lift your spirits and you will soar like an eagle again.

Love your King,
Who will restore all that has been stolen from you.

The Lord hears His people when they call to Him
for help, He rescues them from all their troubles.
Psalm 34:17, NLT

HIS PRINCESS IN ACTION

*Then Jesus said, "Come to me, all of you who are weary
and carry heavy burdens, and I will give you rest."*
Matthew 11:28, NLT

Now give Him those burdens you carry by writing them in a letter to your Lord who loves you and wants to carry this load for you ...

_____

_____

_____

_____

_____

_____

_____

_____

_____

_____

_____

_____

_____

_____

_____

A Treasure of Truth

Whatever you are concerned or worried about right now I want you to stop and say this truth to yourself.....

"He is God...and I am Not!"

> *'Not by might nor by power, but by my Spirit,'*
> *says the LORD Almighty.*
> Zech. 4:6, NIV

Next Step...

Now it's time to let go of anything that is holding you back from the glorious future your King has for you. (If that means crying out to him or confession of hidden hurts, do it now and experience for yourself a real and refreshing cleansing of your soul!)

_____

_____

_____

_____

_____

HIS PRINCESS PRAYER

Dear Abba Father,

Wipe away my tears once again. Lord, help me to trust You and cry out to You. Even though I can not see You, I am taking a step of faith and giving You all my fears, tears, and disappointments. Release me and help me cry out to You so I can be free as You love me back to life again.

I pray in Jesus' name, amen.

Love,
Your Daughter who longs to be healed and held by You.

F.R.**E**.E.D.O.M.

Enter into His presence with praise and prayer

After you find the root and run to the King with your hurts, the next step toward freedom is to enter into His presence by praising Him through your pain.

> *"He has given me a new song to sing, a hymn of praise to our God. Many will see what he has done and be astounded; they will put their trust in the Lord"*
> Psalm 40:3, NLT

HIS PRINCESS DEVOTION

*I*n the fairy tales that I've heard, the princesses always seem to maintain hope in the middle of the most miserable circumstances. They somehow know that their prince will rescue them—and he always does. Our God is our place of rest, our safe place. When we are in His presence, He will restore our minds, our bodies, and our souls. Acts 16 gives us a beautiful illustration of what can happen when we praise our Prince in the midst of our trials and tribulations. Paul and Silas, two faithful men of God, were unjustly thrown into prison for boldly sharing God's message of hope. They could have been angry at God for not protecting them, they could have been worried about their future or their very lives, or they could have chosen to trust the King in their trials and praise Him despite their circumstances. Paul and Silas chose to praise God from a cold, ugly prison cell with songs of praise.

According to Scripture, other prisoners heard and listened as these faithful followers sang songs of love to their Lord. Suddenly there was a great earthquake, and the prison was shaken to its foundation. The doors flew open, and the chains fell off of every prisoner. (Something supernatural happens when, in the midst of battle, we choose to offer a sacrifice of praise to our King!) Not only were Paul and Silas set free from their chains, but every prisoner who was listening and watching their reaction to a bad situation was set free as well.

This prison scene shows us that our reactions to life affect more than us. As a matter of fact, the way we react is the key to not only our freedom, but all who are watching.

HIS PRINCESS LOVE LETTER TO YOU

My Princess,

I will never leave you or forsake you my love. I promise you my daughter, when you go through deep waters of great trouble I will be with you. When you are in the fiery furnace of your faith, as I was with my chosen one Daniel in that furnace, I am with you my love. I will be with you always. And, if you will let me fight your battles for you, you will never burn up or burn out. As you learn to walk with me you will experience the peace that passes all understanding. Remember this my beloved, nothing or no one can steal your appointed position without your permission. So stay close to your Daddy and rest in me.

Love,
Your Protector and King.

> *"Do not be afraid, for I have ransomed you. I have called you by name; you are mine. When you go through deep waters, I will be with you. When you go through rivers of difficulty, you will not drown. When you walk through the fire of oppression, you will not be burned up; the flames will not consume you."*
> Isaiah 43:1-2, NLT

A Treasure of Truth
Praise is Not Denying the Problem.
Praise is looking to God as the Power and Solution!

Praise God though your pain in a written letter... right now

_____
_____
_____
_____
_____
_____
_____
_____
_____
_____
_____
_____
_____
_____
_____
_____
_____
_____

A PRINCESS PRAYER OVER YOU

Dear Lord,

*A*s it is written in Exodus 15:2, You Lord, are my sister's strength and her song. Help her to experience the true joy of her salvation. Let her desire to praise You all the days of her life no matter what pain or problems this life brings. Thank You that she can rest in Your loving arms and that You are her faithful Father who always keeps His word.

In Jesus' name I pray for my Sister Princess, amen.

F.R.E.**E.**D.O.M.

Eliminate the enemy's weapons

The devil does not have to destroy us to win...all he has to do is steal our worth by teaching us lies about ourselves and then he has won.

Once you have found the root of your pain or problem, and then made the choice to run to God and enter into His presence by praising Him through any and all healing and deliverance, it is time for you to taste real victory by eliminating all of the enemy's weapons in your life.

HIS PRINCESS DEVOTION

*I*f a police officer came to your door and warned you that your neighbors had just been robbed and killed, you would be on the look out for anything that could let that enemy in your home or near your loved ones. Our King warns us in His Word that there is an enemy after us (John 10:10) and he is out to kill, steal, and destroy us. He also warns us that if we are not careful, we will help him (the devil) accomplish his mission by what we read, watch, and listen to. We will let him destroy our values, our minds, and our children through the modern entertainment we allow in our homes.

Our lives can become louder than the world's influence. We are Princess Warriors of the King and have been given the power and privilege to live a better life. Our Father knows what's best for His daughters. His rules and warnings are for our good and the key to true freedom from depression, confusion and destruction. It is not that our King does not want His daughters to have any fun or entertainment; He wants to protect our minds, our bodies, and our souls from destruction. (If you don't believe this is true take a good look at the fearful, negative and depressed people who have traded their passion for life and peace of mind for a moment's pleasure).

HIS PRINCESS IN ACTION

How foolish are those who manufacture idols. These prized objects are really worthless. The people who worship idols don't know this, so they are all put to shame.
Isaiah 44:9, NLT

What things in your life have become your gods? Pray to God and ask Him to reveal the things that have been controlling you. Write these things down as you hear from the Lord.

_____

_____

_____

_____

_____

_____

_____

_____

_____

_____

_____

_____

Now personalize Isaiah 44:9

How foolish am I if I allow manufactured idols to be my gods. These highly valued objects are really worthless to the call of God on my life. For deep down I know these idols are meaningless and empty. No wonder if I allow myself to worship them I am put to shame.

_____

_____

_____

_____

_____

_____

_____

_____

Treasure of Truth

You are a treasured Daughter of the Highest King! Don't allow any worthless idols to determine your worth or cause you to believe lies about yourself.

HIS PRINCESS IN ACTION

Take this moment right now to write down any lie
have you believed about yourself.

_____

_____

_____

_____

HIS PRINCESS PRAYER

Dear God,

I lay at your feet the lies I have believed and choose
on this day to believe that I am who You say I am.
Please help me to look to You as my mirror. Guard
my mind from ever believing the lies of man over
Your truth, and help me to walk in Your confidence
not my own. Thank you that I do not have to win
Your love and affection for me. What a privilege!

In Jesus' name I pray, amen.

You did not choose Me I chose you!
John 15:16, NLT

Next step towards freedom...

Write down how you feel about yourself after looking through a beauty magazine.

_____

_____

_____

_____

_____

You and I are daughters of the King, and we are to model His true beauty for the world. No one will ever remember these cover girls when their time of fame comes to an end. Get rid of any books or magazines that threaten your identity in Christ and cause you to feel shame about how God made you. Don't allow these worthless idols to determine your worth.

What would the Lord want to have you edit from your collection of books and magazines that steal your identity in Christ and take away your God-given confidence? (Write it down and get rid of it)

_____

_____

_____

_____

_____
_____
_____
_____
_____
_____
_____
_____
_____
_____
_____
_____
_____
_____
_____
_____
_____
_____
_____
_____
_____
_____
_____
_____
_____

I will lead a life of integrity in my own home.
I will refuse to look at anything vile and vulgar.
Psalm 101:2–3, NLT

HIS PRINCESS DEVOTION

Edit what you watch...

*T*he devil does not have to destroy us to win....all he has to do is distract us...and he has won our attention!

We live in a town so small that I think we have only one yellow page. I lived in Southern California and Scottsdale, Arizona, prior to moving to this tiny town in Oregon. Needless to say, there is not a lot to do. So it would be very tempting to get cable TV, but I have a husband, a teenage son, and a seven-year-old daughter.

It occurred to me one day that, if I agreed to pay thirty dollars a month to receive several hundred channels, I would be opening the door of our home to the enemy. I would essentially be inviting him in so that he could attack and undermine the godly values and priorities I'm trying to instill in my children. And he could steal my relationship with my husband, who might easily pay more attention to the television than to our children or me.

As if all that wouldn't be dangerous and damaging enough, my son and husband would be exposed to images of sex, women, and violence over one hundred times an hour as they flipped through the channels. My little daughter would learn to disrespect me as she watched cartoons and sitcoms that portray children as disrespectful, running the household, and with parents as idiots.

Now, I'm not saying that all television is bad. My Jewish family came to know the Lord through Christian television. But why would we pay to allow images in our home that stand for everything we don't? Besides, we have only a very short time to talk with and teach our children, and in the busyness of life we have very little time to be with our husbands. How are we spending this valuable time? Are hours of television going to draw us closer to God, to our loved ones, and to fulfilling our purpose on this planet? Will those hours in front of the television help us reach the next generation and the world around us for Christ?

Today television, computers, and game boxes take up so much time and energy that many young people don't know how to look in a person's eyes and have a conversation. If we let the television teach them how to live, we are setting them up for failure and heartache.

I admit that there are some great television shows I'd like to watch, but I would not trade the time I spend with my family talking and laughing and praying together for the most entertaining program in the world. Sometimes we have to trade what we want at the moment for what we want most. And I have found that exchanging television for time with my family is definitely worth the trade!

Write down the Movies and TV shows you watch... _____

_____

_____

_____

_____

How many hours does your family spend watching TV each day?____

How many hours does your family spend on the computer?____

Now write down how many minutes (let's be real) you spend reading the Bible each day.____

How many minutes a day do you spend praying to God?____

How much quality time do you spend with your family each day?___

Ask yourself, is the entertainment value worth trading time with God and those you love?

_____

Let's become a generation that still says with Godly confidence...

> *As for me and my household, we will serve the Lord.*
> Joshua 24:15, NIV

HIS PRINCESS LOVE LETTER TO YOU

My Princess,

I want you to eliminate all things that carry you away from your royal call and wipe out your dedication to me. If you will take heed to my warning and come to me, I will show you by my Spirit the things that are causing you to feel sad and insecure. Because I am your Father in Heaven, I want to protect you. However my love, I will never force you to follow me. The choice is yours to choose me or the world. Whatever you chose I am only a prayer away when you lose your way.

Love,
Your King who knows what's best for His girl.

HIS PRINCESS PRAYER

Dear Lord,

Please show me what I am reading and watching that is keeping me from You. Help me see what I am allowing in my home for what it is—and then give me the courage and conviction to say no to what I shouldn't be allowing. Grant me the self-discipline to give up whatever You ask me to surrender and, starting today, to read and watch that which will build my faith and character. I pray in faith that You will transform me and cleanse me from the inside out.

In Jesus' name I pray, amen.

Fix your thoughts on what is true and honorable and right, and pure and lovely and admirable. Think about things that are excellent and worthy of praise.
Philippians 4:8, NLT

Treasure Of Truth
Watch **your thoughts**…They become **your words**
Watch **your words**….They become **your actions**
Watch **your actions**….They become **your habits**
Watch **your habits**….They become **your character**
Watch **your character**….it becomes **your legacy**

F.R.E.E.**D**.O.M.

Do What God Tells You...

*I will not remain with you any longer unless you destroy
the things among you that were set apart for destruction.*
Joshua 7:12, NLT

HIS PRINCESS DEVOTION

No weapon formed against us will prosper.....

*U*nless we step out from behind God's shield of protection around us by fighting in our own strength
and our own way!

We cannot continue to make wrong choices and
expect right results. All God's promises come with
a condition (a choice to obey and be blessed or disobey and be cursed). In Deuteronomy 20, Moses
was nearing the end of his life. He had done all that
God had asked him to do. He was not perfect, but
he was committed to the call God had on his life.
Moses had stood up against Pharaoh despite his
fears, and he had led his people out of captivity.
Moses did his best to get the Israelites to obey the
Lord. He wanted them to see God's promises come

to pass. But they chose their way over God's way and then spent forty years of their lives wandering aimlessly in the desert.

Choosing their own way led the children of Israel into a new kind of captivity. They missed their crowning moment in life to do something great, to settle in the Promised Land. Today that generation is remembered for their disobedience. Moses tried to warn God's chosen people one more time before he died: God longs to bless you, but receiving His blessings depends on your willingness to obey His commands.

If we choose to disobey the Lord, we will not experience the fullness of His blessings. But even worse than that, God will lift His shield of protection from us. Moses then goes on to warn us that curses and diseases will come upon us (Deuteronomy 28:15). Just look around you. There are signs of this truth wherever there is rebellion against God and Christians are living their own way instead of His way. This does not mean God does not love us if we disobey Him—His grace and mercy are with us regardless of our actions.

If the Lord wrote Deuteronomy 31:6 in a personal letter just to His Princesses, it would read something like this...

HIS PRINCESS LOVE LETTER TO YOU

My Princess...

I, your King, stand outside the door of your heart and knock. I see you locked up in your private place of pain, but I won't force My way in. I will continue to wait patiently outside until you're ready to let Me come in. I long to hold you in My arms, wipe away your tears, and tenderly encourage you with My love and truth. I will continue to knock even when you turn a deaf ear. I won't stop calling to you from outside the door of your prison of pain. You do not have to answer, but I won't give up because I love you. I know your heart's cry is for the wholeness and healing that only I can bring. It's not too late, My princess. Today you can unlock the door in the darkened room of your heart and let Me come in. Like warm light and a gentle breeze, I will refresh and nourish your soul.

Love,
Your King and your Key to Freedom.

HIS PRINCESS IN ACTION

God's way does not always make sense in our eyes...

Imagine when Moses was up against that Red Sea. As he approached the edge of the water, he saw his enemies charging toward him and his people (who God had promised to deliver) on one side, and a sea of hopelessness on the other. It looked like the end for God's people. Can you imagine his thoughts?

What is your sea of hopelessness?

_____

_____

_____

_____

What does God want you to do about your circumstance according to His Word? (Not someone's opinion!)

_____

_____

_____

_____

_____

_____

HIS PRINCESS PRAYER

Dear Jesus,

I want to be blessed and shielded by Your protection. I confess to You right now that I have done some things my way, and I want to choose Your way today. Show me anything in me that I need to repent of and any situation that I am not handling Your way. I am ready to break through to a blessed life in You. Please lead me by Your Holy Spirit on the path of righteousness and do in me whatever You need to do to prepare me for the work You have for me. I want to become a woman of character so I can complete the call You have on my life. Because I love you Lord…today I choose life… Your way!

In Your name, I pray, amen.

I call heaven and earth as witnesses today against you,
that I have set before you life and death, blessing and cursing;
therefore choose life, that both you and your descendants may live;
Deuteronomy 30:19, NKJV

HIS PRINCESS IN ACTION

Be still and pray. Write down whatever the Holy
Spirit reveals to you to do and DO IT!!! Find freedom and blessing from your Daddy in Heaven.

_____
_____
_____
_____
_____
_____
_____
_____
_____
_____
_____
_____
_____
_____
_____
_____
_____
_____
_____
_____

Treasure of Truth

We Will Not Experience ...

Peace without... Trusting Him
Power without... Praying to Him
Victory without... Accountability
Wisdom without... Reading His Word
Blessings or break through... Without Obedience
A Crown without the Price Jesus paid at the Cross!
God's Love is Unconditional...His Promises are NOT!

It's our choices not chance that will determine our destiny.
Our obedience or disobedience to God will carve the
future of our country and entire generation.

> *I lay the sins of the parents upon their children; the entire*
> *family is affected—even children in the third and fourth*
> *generations of those who reject me. But I lavish unfailing*
> *love for a thousand generations on those who love me and*
> *obey my commands.*
> Exodus 20:5b-6, NLT

F.R.E.E.D.**O**.M.

Operate in your Appointed Position

Your passion and what you do well is your appointed position. If we were on an actual battlefield fighting a physical war, winning would depend in large part on each of us doing what we were trained to do. Can you imagine putting someone on the front lines who didn't know how to use a gun? Or how about letting fellow soldiers rather than doctors perform surgeries on the wounded?

We aren't able to see the weapons used against us in the spiritual realm, but God warns us that they are there. The best way we can fight the fight effectively is to take our appointed place on the battlefield.

God created you with a gift that He wants you to give to the world. The day you received your new life in Christ, that gift was awakened and empowered by the Holy Spirit for use in God's Kingdom. Your passion and what brings you to life inside is your appointed position.

HIS PRINCESS LOVE LETTER TO YOU

My Precious Princess,

I have given you the gift of eternal life, but My giving does not stop there. Inside of you is a supernatural surprise—a gift waiting for you to unwrap. Yes, it's there, My love. It's hidden within dreams waiting to be pursued, but it's also swallowed up by daily distractions and drowned out by life's disappointments and uncertainties. Come ask Me about it, My daughter, and I will show you how to unwrap what I placed inside of you before the day you were born. You will find your gift in the place that brings you the greatest joy and in the work you most love to do. Using your gift will satisfy your soul, but this gift is not just for you. I have placed it in you to give away while you shine on earth for me. Don't waste another day trying to be someone you were not created to be. Instead ask me now, and I will reveal to you who you really are and what you are destined to do for My kingdom.

Love,
Your King, who has an appointed position for you.

God has given each of you a gift from his great variety of
spiritual gifts. Use them well to serve one another.
1 Peter 4:10, NLT

Find your Position...Start with a prayer

HIS PRINCESS PRAYER

Dear God,

I am ready to let You by the power of Your love and Holy Spirit, unwrap the gift You placed inside of me. Show me my appointed position in this life according to Romans 12:6-8, and anoint me to use this gift; not to bring glory to myself but to bring glory to You and to bless as many as You allow me to with the gift you have given me. Lord, also help me walk in Your confidence and not my own as I step onto the battlefield of life. Place me where I am most effective according to Your plan and timing, not my own.

In Jesus' name I pray, amen.

Notes: _____

_____

_____

_____

_____

HIS PRINCESS SPIRITUAL GIFTS

We have different gifts, according to the grace given us.
If a man's gift is prophesying, let him use it in proportion
to his faith. If it is serving, let him serve; if it is teaching,
let him teach; if it is encouraging, let him encourage; if it is
contributing to the needs of others, let him give generously;
if it is leadership, let him govern diligently; if it is showing
mercy, let him do it cheerfully.
Romans 12:6-8, NIV

Princess Prophet

If you have the gift of prophecy, then you are naturally strong in your convictions. You can give us courage to stand for righteousness and lead us to victory as you boldly stand up against the enemy of our souls by exposing sin. You are an excellent example of what it means to fear God more than man.

Princess Server

If you have the gift of service, you naturally see needs the rest of us don't see. You know how to take care of others, and you find and spread joy in helping make caring things happen. You are an excellent example of how Jesus wants us to serve one another.

Princess Teacher

If you have the gift of teaching, you are the watchdog of the Christian army. You can discern truth, you can teach us, and you can help us better understand the King's truth. We could not survive the battle without you. We could not obey our King's commands if you did not teach us how to get right with God. You are an excellent example of how to live with deep conviction in our hearts.

Princess Encourager

If you have the gift of encouragement, you are our spiritual cheerleader. We need you especially when someone or something has wounded us. You help us keep fighting the good fight. You remind us of the King's eternal truths, and you help us soar to new heights in life in Him. You are an excellent example of how to build each other up in our faith.

Princess Giver

If you have the gift of giving, you help supply our spiritual and practical needs. You also teach us to be generous, and you help us discover the true joy of giving. Your gift is beyond far-reaching and life-changing charitable organizations, and you have a great desire to see God's kingdom advance. You are an excellent example of what it means to invest in eternity.

Princess Leader

If you have the gift of leadership, you get things done; you make things happen. Without you, we would not have retreats, conventions, or order in the church. You see the big picture, you know how to direct people where they can best serve, and you help dreams become reality. You are an excellent example of what it means to put our purpose into action.

Princess Mercy

If you have the gift of mercy, you are part of the nervous system of the body of Christ. You feel our pain, you share our burdens, you listen to us with your whole heart, and you show us how to serve others deeply. When you share your gift, you show us God's mercy, and you help us get through life's tough times. You are an excellent example of how to show God's tenderness to the world.

I pray that you have found your gift—and may you use it to bless others rather than impress others. And may you never again doubt that you are called for a Kingdom purpose.

HIS PRINCESS IN ACTION

Where are you the most effective? Think for a moment about something you love to do, something that energizes and gives you joy and that you do well. (ie: organizing, directing, serving, writing, teaching, singing, work with children, decorating, counseling, coordinating, hosting, cooking, volunteering).

Write down what you do well or love to do...

_____

_____

_____

_____

Now write out something you can do now to bless others (serve, sing, children's ministry, choir, street ministry, baby sit for a single mom, be a Sunday greeter at church, prepare meals; anything that you can do to bring glory to your Daddy in heaven by your acts kindness)

_____

_____

_____

_____

HIS PRINCESS PRAYER OVER YOU

Dear God,

I lift my sister in Christ up before Your throne in Heaven. As it is written in Your word (Eph. 3:20) may You do in her life exceedingly, abundantly more than she would dare to ask, hope or dream for. May she find what You have predestined her to do to further Your Kingdom. And on this day may she trade self-confidence for God-confidence to walk through this life in divine purpose and total peace about who You created her to be.

In Jesus' name I pray, amen.

F.R.E.E.D.O.**M.**

Move on

Forget the former things; do not dwell on the past.
See, I am doing a new thing! Now it springs up; do
you not perceive it? I am making a way in the desert
and streams in the wasteland.
Isaiah 43:18-19, NIV

HIS PRINCESS DEVOTION

Finally, I confessed all my sins to you and stopped trying to hide my guilt. I said to myself, "I will confess my rebellion to the LORD." And you forgave me! All my guilt is gone.
Psalm 32:5, NLT

I thought I was totally free from the shame of my past until one day after I became pregnant with my first child. On that afternoon the shame surfaced again—and quite powerfully.

My husband and I were so excited about going to the doctor to confirm that yes, we were going to have a baby. There I was, lying on the doctor's table, when he asked me if I wanted to hear my baby's heartbeat. I said, "How is that possible? I'm only six weeks pregnant." I had been told—wrongly!—that babies don't have heartbeats until they are at least twenty weeks old.

The doctor put the stethoscope to my tummy, and for the very first time I heard the beat of my son's heart. I began to cry.... My husband thought I was crying tears of joy. However, the truth is that I was crying tears of pain and regret—even terror!

How could such a miraculous moment bring that reaction? Distant memories flooded my mind. I choked back my tears as I recalled an afternoon twelve years earlier. I was only sixteen at the time, but lying on that doctor's table suddenly made it feel as if it were yesterday. One stupid mistake with a guy, and I had found myself pregnant. An abortion, the doctor told me, was the right thing to do, "It's only been six weeks. It's not a baby. It doesn't even have a heartbeat," he assured me.

Now I was confronted for the first time with the horrifying truth about that long-ago decision—and I was too ashamed to tell my husband. For several more years I lived with such shame and fear that I was sure God would take my son in order to punish me. I didn't know how there was any way I could get right with God for something so wrong, something that had happened so long ago.

My Prince finally rescued me over Easter weekend in 1999. It was Good Friday night, and we were at church. A big wooden cross had been displayed in the sanctuary, and each of us were holding a big nail and a small piece of paper. Then the pastor told the story of Easter unlike I had ever heard it before. When he finished, he invited anyone who was holding on to past sin or shame to write it on the paper, walk forward, pick up a hammer, and nail it to the cross.

I thought, Can my Lord really remove the guilty stains and wipe away my shame? I sat there paralyzed by my fear of what people would think if I walked forward. Finally, I felt the Spirit of God whisper, "Give Me your past. Give Me your shame." I got up and walked toward the cross. The moment I picked up that hammer and drove the nail through my confessed sin, I felt the Lord whisper in my spirit, "This is why I had to die for you—so I could take away all your guilt and shame." At that moment He replaced my past pain with His peace.

After that night, I began to understand that confession is more than just something God requires, some kind of "have-to" that we must deal with. Confession is a gift from God by which He replaces the strongholds of our past sin and shame with blessings of forgiveness and freedom, healing and hope. Today I am free from the fear of God's punishment, not because of anything I can do in my own power, but because my Prince paid the price for my sin. I am forgiven!

If you are holding onto something, maybe it's time for you to look at the cross as more than a symbol of your Savior's death. When our Lord died and rose again, He broke forever the power of sin on our lives.

Right now, take a moment and invite the Lord to search your heart for any unresolved sin from your past that continues to torment you. Don't wait until the wedding day! You can experience cleansing and freedom from this day forward!

> *He has removed our sins as far from us as*
> *the east is from the west.*
> Psalm 103:12, NLT

HIS PRINCESS LOVE LETTER TO YOU...

My princess,

*F*orget the former things! All have sinned and fallen short of My glory. If you've confessed your sins, I've forgiven them, so move on! I gave My life so you could be free from your past and live a new life in Me. Forgive those who have hurt you, and most important, forgive yourself. There is no wrong great enough to keep Me from redeeming you. Read My Word, My love. All My chosen ones have made mistakes and have gone through trials. I was with them, and I am with you today. I am ready to do a new thing in you, so trust Me to work out the things that have gone wrong in the past. It's time for you to move forward and do what I sent you here to do.

Love,
Your Savior, Jesus.

Therefore, if anyone is in Christ, he is a new creation;
the old has gone, the new has come!
2 Corinthians 5:17, NIV

Move on from insecurity

Queen Esther…had to move on from her identity as a powerless orphan and accept God's call to be queen. If she had focused on how unqualified she was to reign, she would have missed the opportunity to save the Jewish people and be a part of God's great eternal plan for His chosen ones.

Move on from your past mistakes

King David…had to move on from his sins of adultery and murder. He cried out to God and received His forgiveness. God is so full of grace that He made something good out of David's bad choice by giving him and Bathsheba King Solomon once they repented and moved on.

Move on from guilt

The Apostle Peter…had to move on when he failed to stand up for his Savior. Even though he loved Jesus passionately, Peter denied Him not once, not twice, but three times. If Peter had not accepted God's forgiveness, then he might have spent his entire life paralyzed by guilt rather than helping other Jews realize that Jesus was their long-awaited Messiah.

When we let guilt keep us paralyzed from living out our purpose we are saying by our actions that the cross was not enough to set us free from guilt from our past mistakes. Praise be to our God, we are a new creation.

As far as the east is from the west is how far He has removed our sins from us—and remembers them no more. Do not let the devil whisper lies that you are still guilty—let your Lord whisper His truth that you are totally forgiven and a brand-new creation in Christ.

Move on from Pride

The Apostle Paul...pride could have kept Paul from his call. But, God loved him so much that physical blindness humbled him, and persecution and pain enabled him to share the gospel and build up Christ's church. After only some of his many beatings, imprisonments, and other hardships, Paul could have said, "I don't deserve all this," but then he would have missed all that God had created him for and called him to. Paul had the awesome privilege of teaching and equipping the Gentiles in his day—and, through his many New Testament writings, us centuries later—for a life of holiness.

**Don't let your past torment you...let it teach you.
Leave the past where it belongs...at the cross**

*For you know that when your faith is tested, your
endurance has a chance to grow. So let it grow, for
when your endurance is fully developed, you
will be perfect and complete, needing nothing.*
James 1:3–4, NLT

HIS PRINCESS IN ACTION

Write down what you need to move on from...

_____
_____
_____
_____
_____
_____
_____
_____
_____
_____
_____
_____
_____
_____
_____
_____
_____
_____
_____
_____
_____
_____

HIS PRINCESS LOVE LETTER TO YOU

My love,

I willingly gave My life here on earth and died for you. I went to a cross as your King so that your sins would be forgiven and so you would receive a crown. Not just any crown, but the crown of everlasting life. If you refuse to receive the gift of forgiveness that comes from Me, then you are saying My death isn't enough to cover your sin. Please, My princess, let go of your guilt and forgive yourself and those who have hurt you. In due time I will repay those who hurt you if they don't repent and do what is right. In the meantime you are free…you are forgiven. Once you've confessed your sin to Me, I cast it into the sea of My forgetfulness—never to see or remember it again. So let go and live a free and full life, My precious one.

Love,
Your King, Jesus.

HIS PRINCESS PRAYER

Let's seal this FREEDOM with a final prayer to our Lord and walk out of our private prisons once and for all so we can fight the good fight as His Princess Warriors!

Let's become all we desire to be so we can experience all our Father has for us in this life!

Dear Jesus,

choose on this day to surrender my past, my pain, and my problems to you. I ask you to help me see your plan for my freedom. Give me wisdom and courage to walk through all of life's battles with You. I pray in faith, believing that You have already won my freedom for me and trusting You to fight for me and give me victory in every area of my life. I love You, and I thank You for all You have already done for me and all that You will do for me.

In Your name I pray, amen.

Be strong and courageous. Do not be afraid or terrified because of them, for the LORD your God goes with you; he will never leave you nor forsake you."
Deuteronomy 31:5-7, NIV

REFLECTION

Find the Root
Run to God
Enter into His presence with Praise and Prayer
Eliminate the enemy's weapons
Do what God Tells You!
Operate in your appointed position
Move on!

A CLOSING PRAYER FOR YOU...

I want to personalize and pray 2 Timothy 4:7 over your life right now...

I pray for your complete freedom and strength to finish strong. May you, my Sister Princess, fight the good fight and finish the race set before you. May nothing hinder you from keeping your faith; and may you never forget the crown of life that is in store for you that will be given to you personally on the great and glorious day of our Lord's return. May you walk through the rest of this life in His confidence, and may our Father in Heaven be ever present in your heart, mind, and soul.

In Jesus' name I pray, amen.

I have fought the good fight, I have finished the race, I have kept the faith. Now there is in store for me the crown of righteousness, which the Lord, the righteous Judge, will award to me on that day—and not only to me, but also to all who have longed for his appearing.
2 Timothy 4:7, NIV

His Princess™ Retreat
—WORKBOOK—

Session Two

GROUP DISCUSSION

Royal Relationships

The Art of Loving One Another

1. Read this scripture out loud to the group.

> *If it is possible…as far as it depends on you…*
> *Be at peace with everyone.*
> Romans 12:18 (NIV)

2. Have each person answer below what has God revealed to you about relationships through this teaching?

_____

_____

_____

_____

_____

_____

_____

_____

_____

_____

3. Read His Princess Love Letter to the group.

My Princess,

*L*et Me teach you how to love others and receive love. I am not a God of condemnation but of divine healing and restoration. Come to Me My love and let Me examine your heart. I will never turn my back on you no matter what you have said or done. If you will follow My example and choose My way I will bless your relationships abundantly. You will become the royal example of leading others back into real relationships that bring joy and fulfillment. You can not do this in your own strength, but My spirit in you can do a great and mighty work in your heart and the hearts of others.

Love,
Your King who has covered you.

4. Pray for one another's relationships without sharing details (just cover each other).

HIS PRINCESS PERSONAL STUDY TIME

Royal Relationships

Two people are better off than one, for they can help each
other succeed. If one person falls, the other can reach out and
help. But someone who falls alone is in real trouble.
Ecclesiastes 4:9–10, NLT

Mother Theresa was once asked, "How can we re-store peace to our world?" Her answer was sim-ply this, "Go home and learn to love one another." When she was asked what the worst disease facing mankind was, this tiny woman, who had spent her life in sacrificial service ministering in Calcutta to the sick and the dying, answered that the greatest disease was loneliness especially in America.

Maybe our comforts and conveniences are getting in the way of the very thing we need most…one another.

Loneliness, like cancer, may not manifest any symp-toms at first. We suffer on the inside but appear to be fine on the outside. We smile to people at work, we sing in the pew at church, and we do a good job keeping our 'life is great and I'm happy' look on our face. Yet, if we were really honest with ourselves, many of us would say, "I feel so alone." Why do we suffer in quiet, lonely desperation? Maybe we don't want to appear weak or needy.

Instead, we choose to stay isolated. We create an image that says, "I am secure on my own." The enemy of our soul loves it when we do this. In fact, he tries to separate us from other people. That is one of his most important and often unrecognized strategies. When a lion is hungry, the king of beasts doesn't go after the whole herd. He can't defeat a herd, and he doesn't even try. Instead, he goes after an isolated animal. Likewise, the devil tries to separate an unsuspecting victim from the body of believers. His goal is to isolate the weak because he sees past the painted smile on our face. We might as well paint a bulls-eye on our chest and say, "Come and get me, Satan! I'm alone."

HIS PRINCESS DEVOTION

What makes our hearts melt when we sit in the theater and watch a great love story? It's not the hero's physical strength or his beloved's beauty. You and I are drawn to the power of true love and its inexplicable ability to prevail despite tragedy and hardship (often the greater the conflict the greater the love).

A problem comes though, when we get accustomed to seeing relational problems solved in the time it takes to eat a bag of popcorn and drink a soda. Our hero and his beauty have less than two hours to defeat the dragons and overcome unspeakable challenges (even less if we're watching a situation comedy on TV, where relational conflicts magically resolve themselves in less than thirty minutes!). You and I are not going to magically resolve any relationship in our own wisdom, and definitely not in less than two hours. However, the Author of love, our Prince of Peace, has written a script. His Word on real-life royal relationships can lead us to the happy ending we long for!

Many of us have been wounded by someone and it is hard to let go of that pain.

Let's take a moment and look at King David's example of handling a fierce King Saul who once loved David, but grew bitterly jealous and envious of the call God had on the future King's life. David was running from a man who was trying to hurt, hinder and even kill him. Yet David, in God's strength, was able to resist the temptation to kill his enemy when he came upon the sleeping King Saul. From a human perspective David had good reason to kill Saul. He had made David's life miserable and was now seeking to kill him; Saul was after David without a just reason. Even Saul's son Jonathan took David's side during the hunt. But David, the future anointed king, did something much greater than take revenge; He deferred to God's will and obeyed the command not to strike down the man God had placed on the throne. In other words, He did what his God wanted Him to do.

Treasure of Truth
Care more about God's will than your rights,
and you will win victory.

Many of us will never experience the magnitude of God's great call on our lives until we give revenge, regret, and our rights back to the Lord.

Notes: _____

_____

_____

_____

_____

_____

_____

_____

_____

_____

_____

_____

_____

_____

_____

_____

_____

_____

_____

HIS PRINCESS IN ACTION

*I*s there a King Saul in your life—someone you need to leave to God's care even though you have real reasons to act in revenge? Follow King David's example and let God deal with those who have caused you pain and suffering. If you will do what God wants you to do, you will find the freedom that comes along with doing what is right in God's sight. He will deal with those who have hurt His daughters!

Write a letter to your Lord and give that person to the Him right now...

_____

_____

_____

_____

_____

_____

_____

_____

_____

_____

Take comfort in these words from our Almighty and Just Father in heaven:

> Do not take revenge, my friends, but leave room for God's wrath, for it is written: "It is mine to avenge; I will repay," says the Lord.
> Romans 12:19, NIV

The Art of Loving One Another

Let's do our part to reinstate peace in our relationships as we establish God's will and God's way. Be open to how the Lord leads as we go through the following relational rules that our Father in Heaven has established for His Daughters.

> "It is not good for the man to be alone."
> Genesis 2:18, NIV

At every step of His creative efforts, God pronounced His handiwork "good." Isn't it interesting that the first thing that wasn't good, in God's estimation, was Adam standing alone in the Garden? "It is not good for the man to be alone." This verse in Genesis isn't just about marriage. This verse is about relationships. God made us relational—to need one another, to experience the true joy of relationship.

The problem is many of us don't know how to give love or receive love, so we close the door of our hearts and isolate ourselves from the true source of life and love. We separate ourselves from the herd and, to mix metaphors, become like a pond in the wilderness. No fresh water comes in, and no water leaves, so we become stagnant. Eventually our isolation becomes unhealthy for us and for those who need us—and that isolation can become deadly.

Wherever the river flows, life will flourish.
Ezekiel 47:9, The Message

The beauty of the royal relationship between Jonathan and David is that they did not let the dark spirit of jealously, disappointment, discouragement, pride, or family ties destroy their God-ordained friendship. And that's a key point:

Royal relationships happen when we care more about God's will for one another than about our rights or our way.

Anyone can hang in there when all is going well! The tough times—the times that call for sacrifice—give us the opportunity to prove that we are real friends.

HIS PRINCESS PRAYER

Dear God,

I confess that I have not had the right heart to have royal relationships. Please forgive me for my selfish motives, and remove my fear of getting hurt. Teach me how to have more joy from giving than receiving, and show me how to be the type of friend I desire to have. Open my eyes that I may see people as You do, and give me the heart to love others the way You do.

In Jesus' name I pray, amen.

Notes: _____

_____

_____

_____

_____

_____

_____

HIS PRINCESS IN ACTION

I know how hard it is to look honestly at ourselves because our natural reaction is to look at others or to justify our actions. In order to master the art of real relationships, we have to clean the canvas in our hearts, get right with others, and real with ourselves and God. Only then will we be able to grow into the woman we want to become. I have found from my own mistakes that it is never too late to change. No one is perfect. We all make relational mistakes. Let's use those mistakes as tutors to become better at loving one another.

Ask Yourself...

How do your friends and family feel about themselves after they have spent time with you?

Do they feel...envious...inferior...depressed... exhausted...discouraged...depressed... anxious to get away from you?

Or do they feel...loved...accepted... encouraged...refreshed...blessed?

Those who refresh others will themselves be refreshed
Proverbs 11:25, NLT

HIS PRINCESS CHALLENGE

*I*f you really want to grow in your relational skills ask others how you make them feel about themselves when they spend time with you and give them *(your family, friends and co-workers)* freedom to be honest.

Write out some changes you want to make about the way you talk to and treat those closest to you *(Write names and the change you want to make)*

Family_____

_____

_____

_____

Friends _____

_____

_____

_____

Spouse _____

_____

_____

_____

Children _____

_____

_____

_____

_____

Others _____

_____

_____

_____

Pray and ask God...
Is there is anyone you need to go to and ask FOR-GIVNESS from for the way you made them feel?

_____

_____

_____

_____

Let's learn to care for each other!
Do not withhold good from those who deserve it
when it's in your power to help them.
Proverbs 3:27, NLT

HIS PRINCESS DEVOTION

*D*o I care more about impressing or about blessing?
God commands us not to withhold good when we are
able to help those who are in need. Too often, though,
we do all we can for those who don't need our acts of
service. When we do this, we burn ourselves out and
become bitter toward those who don't appreciate our
expression of love. There are two reasons we displace
our love like this, and both of them are rooted in self,
not in selfless. Let's examine our hearts.

Do I serve to gain attention and approval of others?
This is a question we should all ask ourselves. Is
this for God's glory or my own?

If we do indeed spend our entire life caring and
serving others in an attempt to validate our worth
and to bring attention to ourselves, sadly, the enemy

of our soul will put people in our path who use and abuse us. We will always get hurt when we give out of selfish ambition or motives. Furthermore, we will see no fruit from those friendships because our hearts won't be in a place for receiving love.

Giving of ourselves is useless if our motive is to bring glory to anyone other than our King. The truth is that no one will ever see our hearts as God does. He also gives great rewards to His girls when we do things for His glory not our own.

If you see yourself in the above description, then I invite you to pray this prayer.

HIS PRINCESS PRAYER

Dear Jesus,

I confess that I do good things to bring glory to me and gain the approval of others. I have wasted a lot of time doing things for others to get them to like me. Please release me now from giving people the power to define my value. Please teach me to look to You to validate my worth. Carve in my memory the price You paid for me on that cross. Let Your love and approval be all that I need.

In Your name I pray, amen.

Notes_____

_____

_____

_____

_____

_____

_____

Do I give in order to get something from others?
Caring for others makes for close relationships, but our motive for caring cannot be that of getting someone to love us or give us what we want. That is not the road toward a relationship that nurtures and grows us. And if we choose that road, the enemy will put people in our path that will treat us like slaves starved for affection. Think about those relationships where you can never measure up to the other person's expectations, and the more you try to, the more they reject you. You either become obsessed with trying to get them to love you, or you start playing their games and pretending that you don't care. Often you resort to doing things to make them feel the pain you feel. These approaches are not God's plan for relationships; they are mind games that nobody wins. If you are playing 'Relational Battleship' with someone—whether men, parents, or girlfriends—you will not win the love you're after.

If this description reminds you of yourself, I invite you to pray with me for strength and courage to stop playing these destructive games forever.

HIS PRINCESS PRAYER

Dear God,

I confess I have allowed others to play dangerous games with my mind and emotions in order to try to win their affection. I ask you to show me where I'm doing that right now in any relationship I'm in. I need you to set me free from my vain efforts to win love; I ask you to free me to feel Your love so that I will be able to love others. Lord, let me know how to walk off the game field and teach me, by Your Holy Spirit, how to have real-life royal relationships.

In Jesus' name I pray, amen.

Notes_____
_____
_____
_____
_____
_____

HIS PRINCESS IN ACTION

Write out whatever the Lord has revealed to you about your motives in a prayer of confession with a commitment to change.

_____ .
_____
_____
_____
_____
_____

Write out whatever the Lord has revealed to you about caring for others.

_____
_____
_____
_____
_____
_____
_____
_____
_____

Let's start covering one another

Read a proverb from the wisest king who ever lived.

He who covers over an offense promotes love,
but he who repeats the matter separates close friends.
Proverbs 17:9, NIV

HIS PRINCESS DEVOTION

*T*hese words offer a wealth of wisdom about the art of loving one another. We all find ourselves tempted to repeat a juicy matter of interest (also known as gossip!), but if we are going to have the deep, meaningful relationships we long for, then we are going to have to choose to cover our friends' frailties and loved ones' mistakes by keeping details about their personal lives to ourselves. No one benefits when we expose one another's weaknesses to other people. In fact, everyone loses.

I've learned the hard way that it takes a lot more character to cover over someone's sins and failings than it does to expose them. Remember that the enemy's mission is to keep us from being close to one another. If we aren't careful with our words, we will actually be helping him separate us from one another. When people share a deeply personal part of their life with you, they are giving you the great privilege of allowing you into their private world. They are saying that they trust and value you enough to share secrets of their heart. When we understand this truth about trust, we will want to treasure and protect the things we know about one another rather than expose them for everyone to see.

Sometimes those who are dear to our hearts need love the most when they deserve it the least.

Let's pray...

HIS PRINCESS PRAYER

Dear God,

Please forgive me for not covering over the offenses of my family and friends, and convict me when I am inadvertently helping the enemy destroy my relationships with them. Teach me to treasure the truth about them that they entrust to me. Open my eyes to see the people in my life the way You see them, and enable me to extend to them the same grace that You give to me.

In Jesus' name I pray, amen.

Most important of all continue to show deep love for each other for love covers a multitude of sins...
1 Peter 4:8, NLT

HIS PRINCESS IN ACTION

*D*on't waste another day if you have exposed or un-covered someone who trusted you. Go to them to-day and ask their forgiveness so that you can receive God's blessing of peace of mind. Even if they do not forgive you, God will bless you for doing what is right in His sight. (If you can not get to them in person write or email a sincere apology.)

Write out the name(s) of those who you need to go to. Be sure and pray for them before you go and see them.

1._____
2._____
3._____
4._____

Let's learn to connect with each other.

HIS PRINCESS DEVOTION

There is an art to communication

All of us have felt the pain of being misunderstood. It's discouraging to express ourselves in love only to see our words become the very thing that separates us from the one we care about. I think we see this especially in marriage: Rather than drawing closer to your spouse, your choice of words can painfully tear you away from each other. God's Word warns us that the power of life and death is in our tongues; we can heal or hurt someone with a word. The key to mastering the art of communication is by remembering just how powerful our words really are.

Also powerful and very damaging is our silence. Communication breaks down if we choose not to communicate at all. Maybe we have shut down, not wanting to be heard, seen or noticed, because we have been put down most of our lives. I know the pain of being put down, but I also know that the Master Artist can take those wounds and use them to turn you into a beautiful, compassionate woman who is careful with her words. The King's healing touch can bring you back to life so you don't have to hide any longer. He loves you and He will do whatever it takes to help you become the princess He wants you to be...but you must go to Him!

HIS PRINCESS PRAYER

Dear God,

Sometimes I am afraid to speak because I'm afraid I'll say the wrong words. Please remove my fear and replace it with faith in You. Fill my heart with Your love and my mouth with Your words. Give the people I'm talking to the ability to know my heart even when my words come out wrong. I thank You for the privilege You have given me to pray, and I trust You to guide my lips to speak words of Your love.

In Jesus' name, amen.

HIS PRINCESS IN ACTION

Write down what the Lord reveals to you about
how you communicate with others.

_____

_____

_____

_____

_____

_____

_____

_____

_____

_____

_____

_____

_____

_____

_____

_____

_____

_____

_____

_____

HIS PRINCESS DEVOTION

Get real in your relationships

We've all probably experienced the frustration of a fake friendship when we act like "Barbies with a Bible." Those relationships amount to little more than wasted words and wasted time, and often we become even more plastic as a result of those insincere connections. Barbie looks perfect on the outside, but we all know she is plastic and totally empty on the inside. His princesses are far from empty on the inside. Communication breaks down when we offer, so to speak, only a black-and-white copy of ourselves rather than the original. No one values what isn't real. But too many of us try so hard to say what we think will make us look good rather than giving the gift of genuineness and transparency. With that effort we close the door to real-life royal relationships.

It's time to take off our masks and let the Lord reveal Himself through the way we communicate with each other. Then we will find what we are longing for …a real connection of the heart.

HIS PRINCESS PRAYER

Dear God,

*H*elp me to communicate in a way that is real. Take off my mask and replace it with your true reflection in me. Let me be as real as King David was. Set me free from myself and let me speak like royalty—with kindness and respect, with self-control and affirmation. Let every one of my conversations be rich in the traits that matter to You. Set me free to be the real me.

In Jesus' name I pray, amen.

HIS PRINCESS IN ACTION

Take a moment to think about your relationships. Ask God to show you which ones are not genuine and which are of real value. Write them down.

_____

_____

_____

_____

There is a real art to communication. Take the test below and find out what picture you are painting of yourself to others with your words.

Take a Talk Test
When I talk to others I...

* Talk about myself with them asking for info
    (Yes__ No___)
* Constantly correct them or critique them
    (Yes__ No___)
* Boss them around and make them feel dumb
    (Yes__ No___)
* Bring bad news I read or watched that day
    (Yes__ No___)
* Interrupt them while they are trying to talk
    (Yes__ No___)
* Brag and boast about how great I am
    (Yes__ No___)
* Give them the latest gossip news about others
    (Yes__ No___)
*Shut them down if I am not interested in what they are saying
    (Yes__ No___)

Now pray the following Psalm

May the words of my mouth and the thoughts
of my heart be pleasing to you Lord.
Psalm 19:14, NIRV

After praying this Psalm, ASK yourself...
How do others feel after they have spent time talking to me?

Write down how you think they feel after talking with you below: _____
_____
_____
_____
_____
_____
_____
_____

Let's Talk About Godly Gossip...

A troublemaker plants seeds of strife;
gossip separates the best of friends
Proverbs 16:28, NLT

Before you share any information on anyone ask yourself the following questions…

    1. Why am I sharing this information?
    2. Am I willing to have my name used as a reference when the information that I shared is repeated?
    3. How will this affect the person I am talking about? (Or who is listening?)

God's Golden Rule for His Princesses

*Do to others what you would have them do to you,
for this sums up the Law and the Prophets.*
Matthew 7:12, NIV

HIS PRINCESS IN ACTION

Write out a prayer of confession if you have gossiped about anyone and get your heart right with God.

_____
_____
_____
_____
_____

Treasure of Truth

If someone gossips to you...
most likely they will gossip about you.

HIS PRINCESS LOVE LETTER FOR YOU

My Princess,

*L*et me teach you how to love others and receive love. I am not a God of condemnation but of divine healing and restoration. Come to Me My love and let Me examine your heart. I will never turn My back on you no matter what you have said or done. If you will follow My example and choose My way, I will bless your relationships abundantly. You will become the royal example of leading others back into real relationships that brings joy and fulfillment. You can not do this in your own strength. Rely on My Spirit in you and you will see that a great and mighty work will be done in your heart and in the heart of others.

Love,
Your King who has covered you.

Reckless words pierce like a sword,
but the tongue of the wise brings healing.
Proverbs 12:18, NIV

HIS PRINCESS PRAYER

Dear God,

Use my tongue to paint a picture of Your love. Give me the right words—Your words—when someone is sharing deep pain. Forgive me for bragging about the blessings You have given me when others are going through a trial. In those situations, use me to make them feel the way You make me feel—loved, accepted, and encouraged.

In Jesus' name I pray, amen.

We need to confront each other
If your brother sins against you,
go and show him his fault,
just between the two of you.
Matthew 18:15, NIV

I praise God for people in my past who have been brave enough to risk our relationship to be open and honest with me about ways I offended them. Many times God puts these people in our path for our personal growth even if they don't remain lifetime friends. And not every friend will be a friend for life. Different seasons of life call for relationships with different people, and relationships themselves have their different seasons. Let me share an example.

HIS PRINCESS DEVOTION

I went through a season in my marriage when I suffered greatly from loneliness and resentment. I wanted so much to be happily married, that I decided to hide from my husband, Steve, whenever he hurt me—and I hid by saying nothing! Many times the men in our lives hurt us without knowing it, but the pain is still very real. I stayed silent for fear that Steve would not understand me and for fear that I would not live "happily ever after". I also wanted to avoid conflict, something I think a lot of us can relate to.

After several years of hiding, I fell completely out of love with Steve. I had built a high and thick wall of unforgiveness and resentment. While that wall was huge to me, it was invisible to Steve. So, when he hit it, he could not understand why I was so cold and distant from him. To make matters worse, I was a Christian speaker and Mrs. United States at the time (a title that spoke of marriage). Needless to say, I was paralyzed by my pain and trapped inside that cold wall of loneliness I had built around myself.

One day another man, a friend Steve and I had led to the Lord, found the key to unlock the door of my heart: He listened to me with his heart and he prayed for me. After three months of listening to and sharing my hidden hurts, this man had captured my heart so much that I wanted to leave my marriage and my ministry. Even though we never had a physical affair, we had an affair of the heart. I knew it was a sin, but I could not stop seeing him. Only when I finally I cried out to God to rescue me from that dangerous place was I freed from the pull of the relationship. God rescued me by sending godly women and men to confront me privately. These men and women were on my ministry's advisory board, and if they had not had the courage to confront me or the compassion to feel my pain and pray for me, I would not be married or in the ministry today.

Confrontation is just as much of a gift as comforting or caring for one another. If we really love one another, we will fix what is broken in our relationships, and we will keep those we know and love from falling into the temptations or the traps of the enemy. Today I am more than just married; I'm in love with my husband more than I ever dreamed possible. When something is not right, I pray for perfect timing to talk to him, and then I talk to him privately. I have learned not to build any more walls around me because walls do not protect us from pain. All they do is imprison us. We become slaves to self-pity and loneliness.

HIS PRINCESS IN ACTION

*J*esus gives us two specific instructions in Matthew 18:15 First, we are to "go privately," and second, we are to "point out the fault." If we choose any other way to resolve conflict than God's way, we will never know the blessings of lasting relationships. Sadly, too often we don't follow God's way.

One big mistake we make is going public with the relational conflict rather than going privately to the person involved. Suddenly everyone knows there is a problem except for the person with whom we have a conflict. This course of action leads to total devastation for many reasons.

1. We have broken trust by taking personal issues public; once trust is broken, reconciliation of that relationship is a much greater challenge.

2. We drag people into a situation that is none of their concern and we influence those people to think wrongly about the person we're in conflict with.

3. We are not loving the person we're in conflict with the way we'd want that person to love us. And we certainly aren't glorifying God with our words or actions.

4. We are showing ourselves not to be trustworthy. If we'll make public a conflict with one person, we'll probably do the same again with another person.

5. We are sinning against our Lord by not handling confrontation His way.

In the second part of Matthew 18:15...
God gives us permission to point out the fault or offense. He doesn't want us to ignore the hurtful things people say and do nor does He want us to keep quiet about the offense. If we choose not to confront the person who has offended us, that offense will be the beginning of a growing wall of bitterness and resentment toward that person. That wall may eventually become so big that neither party involved can scale it, and the relationship will die.

Our silence might seem spiritual and sacrificial, and telling everyone about the offense may seem right because we're reporting the truth. But the book of Proverbs says it best:

> *There is a way which seems right to a man and appears straight before him, but at the end of it is the way of death.*
> Proverbs 14:12, AMP

HIS PRINCESS PRAYER

Dear God,

Show me any past relationships that I have left unresolved. Forgive me for the times I've exposed people rather than confronting them privately. Forgive me for the times when I've chosen to hide my feelings rather than confront the one who offended me. Whatever the situation, and whatever my sin in mishandling it, please help me do what I can to make the relationship right. Give me courage to confront those who have hurt or offended me—and help me to trust You no matter what the outcome of my efforts. Enable me to do the right thing in Your sight.

In Jesus' name I pray, amen.

HIS PRINCESS WARNING

Confrontation is NOT the same as criticism

Confrontation brings restoration, but criticism brings discouragement and pain. If someone in your life is constantly criticizing you, speak up (confront that person!) and ask him or her to stop. If that person continues, then set boundaries in that relationship; limit your contact with that person.

Treasure of Truth

Dear brothers and sisters, if another believer is overcome by some sin, you who are godly should gently and humbly help that person back onto the right path.
Galatians 6:1, NLT

Be careful how you counsel each other

Let the message about Christ, in all its richness, fill your lives. Teach and counsel each other with all the wisdom he gives.
Colossians 3:16, NLT

List some bad counsel you have received that now,
looking back, you realize that counsel was not
from God.

_____

_____

_____

_____

_____

_____

_____

_____

_____

_____

_____

_____

_____

_____

_____

_____

**When counseling each other use God's words…
Not your own!**

TREASURE OF TRUTH

**Opinions are like belly buttons—
everyone has one.**

*But my child be warned there is no end of opinions ready
to be expressed, studying them can go on forever and
become very exhausting*
Ecclesiastes 12:12 (TLB)

*But, my child, let me give you some further advice: Be
careful, for writing books is endless, and much study wears you out.*
Ecclesiastes 12:12 (NLT)

HIS PRINCESS WISDOM

*B*efore you share your secrets with someone or allow
someone to counsel you, I want to caution you to
choose wisely and to look for the following char-
acteristics in your possible candidates. Do not ask
anyone to hold you accountable or counsel you on
an important matter unless you can answer yes to
all of the following questions about them!

1. Is the person's walk with God strong and consistent and does their counsel line up with God's Word?

2. Does this person love you enough to be truthful with you?

3. Can you trust this person to keep your personal matters private?

4. Will this candidate take seriously the job of holding you accountable?

5. Do you feel comfortable being honest and transparent with this person?

6. Will this person in the faith continually pray for you?

7. Will this person make time to call you or meet with you once a week to keep up with what you are doing?

Don't be discouraged if you can't think of a person who can hold you accountable. Instead, continue to pray and ask your Prince to provide the person He knows you need to fulfill your royal call. Remember that He wants you to stay close to Him and to be ready for His return. So you can be sure that if you ask, He will give you that perfect accountability partner in His perfect time. In the meantime, get yourself into a small group at your church.

Notes: _____

_____

_____

_____

_____

_____

_____

_____

_____

_____

_____

_____

HIS PRINCESS PRAYER

Dear Lord,

Please send me the perfect accountability, a person appointed and ordained by You. Enable me to be real with that person about my goals and dreams, my temptations and weaknesses, my sins and my fears. I trust that You will help me finish strong this journey of faith and find me the perfect fit for what I need to walk faithfully with You.

In Jesus' name I pray, amen.

Let's complete the picture
by completing each other

*Just as our bodies have many parts and each part has a
special function, so it is with Christ's body. We are many
parts of one body, and we all belong to each other.*
Romans 12:4-5, NLT

God has placed each person in our path for a different purpose

Make a list of the top five people in your life and
the purpose you have in each other's lives.

Friend _____

Purpose_____

_____

Friend _____

Purpose_____

_____

Friend _____

Purpose_____

_____

Friend _____

Purpose_____

_____

Friend _____

Purpose_____

_____

_____

Too many times we walk away from a God-ordained relationship because all the pieces of that friendship don't
fall into place the way we want or expect them to.

What do you hope to contribute to the above people
on your list?

_____

_____

_____

_____

_____

_____

_____

_____

_____

_____

HIS PRINCESS WISDOM

Final advice regarding royal relationships
Surround yourself with the kind of people you want to be like because we will become like the people with whom we surround ourselves.

HIS PRINCESS IN ACTION

Who are you surrounded by? *(with whom do you spend the majority of your time?)* _____

_____

_____

_____

_____

_____

Do they draw you closer to God? Yes_____ No_____

This verse in Proverbs says it best.

> *He who walks with the wise grows wise,*
> *but a companion of fools suffers harm.*
> Proverbs 13:20, NIV

HIS PRINCESS LOVE LETTER TO YOU

My precious Princess,

*Y*ou never need to hold on to anyone out of fear of being alone. I am with you wherever you are. I am the friend who walks in when the world walks out. I love you beyond description. I know sometimes you don't feel you deserve to be loved, but remember that you don't have to earn My love or affection. I see your heartache. Don't look to anyone but Me, My love. I am the Lover of your soul. I'm the only One who can love you the way you long to be loved. I know you can't see Me, but My Spirit is within you. You can hear Me speak to you through My Word. You can enter into My presence by praise and prayer anytime you wish. So hold on to hope, My beloved. I'm coming soon, and we will live happily ever after throughout eternity.

Love,
Your King who has covered you.

And be sure of this: I am with you always,
even to the end of the age.
Matthew 28:20, NLT

REFLECTION ON ROYAL RELATIONSHIPS

What If...

We fought for each other ...
    and not against each other
We cared for one another...
    and stopped criticizing each other
We spoke life to one another...
    and stopped speaking death
We prayed for each other ....
    and stopped persecuting each other
We completed each other...
    and stop competing with each other

Let's commit to becoming a real family...and love one another with the love of the Lord! As Mother Theresa said that we can restore peace to our world by learning to love one another. Let it start with us!

If it is possible as far as it depends on you ...
Be at peace with everyone, (Amen!)
Romans 12:18, NIV

Session Three

GROUP DISCUSSION

My Prince Will Come

Preparing for that Glorious Day

1. Read the Scriptures below out loud to the group.

> *So we don't look at the troubles we can see now; rather, we
> fix our gaze on things that cannot be seen. For the things
> we see now will soon be gone, but the things
> we cannot see will last forever.*
> 2 Corinthians 4:18, NLT

> *Let us rejoice and be glad and give him glory!
> For the wedding of the Lamb has come,
> and his bride has made herself ready.*
> Revelation 19:7, NIV

2. Have each person in group answer below:
What did God reveal to you through this teaching?

_____

_____

_____

_____

3. Read Isaiah 54:5 out loud to the group.

> *For your Maker is your husband—*
> *the LORD Almighty is his name—*
> *the Holy One of Israel is your Redeemer;*
> *he is called the God of all the earth.*

4. Have each person in group answer below: How does that truth from God's Word make you feel? _____

_____

_____

_____

_____

_____

_____

_____

_____

_____

_____

_____

_____

_____

_____

5. Read the poem and scriptures below out loud to group:

A Beautiful Heart..
That Is Full of His Love and Free to Love Others

*So that Christ may dwell in your hearts through faith;
and that you, being rooted and grounded in love, may
be able to comprehend with all the saints what is the
breadth and length and height and depth, and to
know the love of Christ which surpasses knowledge,
that you may be filled up to all the fullness of God.*
Ephesians 3:17–19, NASB

A Beautiful Mind...
That Is Focused on Your Purpose

*But the plans of the LORD stand firm forever, the
purposes of his heart through all generations.*
Psalm 33:11, NIV

Beautiful Lips...
That Speak Words of Wisdom,
Encouragement, and Life!

*The Sovereign LORD has given me his words of wisdom,
so that I know what to say to all these weary ones.
Morning by morning he wakens me and opens my under
standing to his will.*
Isaiah 50:4, NLT

Beautiful Feet...
That Walk in God's Confidence
and Lead Others to Him

*How beautiful upon the mountains are the feet of him who
brings good news, who proclaims peace, who brings glad
tidings of good things, who proclaims salvation, who says to
Zion, "Your God reigns!"*
Isaiah 52:7, NKJV

Beautiful Hands...
That Reach Out to Those Who Are in Need

*She opens her hand to the poor, yes, she reaches out her filled
hands to the needy [whether in body, mind, or spirit].*
Proverbs 31:20, AMP

Beautiful Eyes...
That See with an Eternal Perspective

*So we don't look at the troubles we can see now; rather, we fix
our gaze on things that cannot be seen. For the things we see
now will soon be gone, but the things we cannot see will last forever.*
2 Corinthians 4:18, NLT

A Beautiful Life ...
That Will Forever Be Remembered

*Praise the LORD! How joyful are those who fear the
LORD and delight in obeying his commands. Their
children will be successful everywhere; an entire
generation of godly people will be blessed. They
themselves will be wealthy, and their good deeds will
last forever.*
Psalm 112:1–3, NLT

6. Have each person in group answer below:
What do you want to be remembered for when
you are in Heaven? _____
_____
_____
_____
_____
_____
_____
_____
_____
_____
_____

7. Have someone close the group in prayer.

Notes: _____

_____

_____

_____

_____

_____

_____

_____

_____

_____

_____

_____

_____

_____

_____

_____

_____

_____

_____

_____

_____

HIS PRINCESS PERSONAL STUDY TIME

My Prince Will Come

Preparing for the Lord's Return

*O*ur Prince is coming to rescue us from the troubles of this world...and our story is not a Disney dream. It is the greatest love story ever told, and it's true! Our Prince loves us so passionately that He gave His life so we can and will live happily ever after. This final session is about getting ready for that glorious day when we finally see Him face-to-face on our wedding day in Heaven. Even now, while you are reading, your Prince is preparing a place just for you.

HIS PRINCESS DEVOTION

The bride-to-be stood motionless, staring in the mirror for what seemed like an eternity. She had worked hard preparing for this moment. Her hair and makeup were a work of art, and her dress was stunning. Never before had she felt so beautiful. But something was missing. Something had gone terribly wrong. Where were her guests? Had she not made it clear to everyone that this day was coming? The greatest day the world would ever know? An open guest book sat beside her—blank. The gift table—empty… except for a stack of unopened letters. Were those the wedding invitations she should have sent out? No, they couldn't be. She was sure she had mailed those weeks ago. The bride fumbled through the pile. Every letter was addressed to her, and each one had been sent from the same person—her Beloved Prince. Of course she recognized his handwriting. She had read his letters before—long ago—but life had kept her so busy that there really hadn't been any time to read his letters. The bride sifted through the pile looking for something without really knowing what. Tears filled her eyes as she read the familiar phrase her Prince had written on the envelope: "I can't wait to see you face to face, my dearest princess! I love you!" A sense of eagerness overcame her, and she began to open the envelope. But just then, she heard the sound of the most beautiful music in the distance more beautiful than she had ever heard before. It was time…the wedding march had begun! She dropped the letter and ran toward the large double doors that opened into the gloriously decorated sanctuary. The anointed sweet music filled the empty hall. She wrestled with these unanswered questions as she slowly walked down the aisle ...Where were her friends? Where was her family? Did she not make it clear that they were invited to be here? Then, suddenly, everything around her seemed to blur as she caught sight of Him.

He stood tall and gentle on the platform at the end of the aisle, patiently and lovingly waiting for His bride to approach. There were no bridesmaids or groomsmen; only her Prince Jesus and what appeared to be stacks and stacks of wedding presents. She had heard that He had prepared many gifts for His bride, but this was truly overwhelming.

She always knew her emotions would run wild on her wedding day, but nothing had prepared her for the intense flood that filled and overflowed her heart at that moment. As she approached her Groom—

her Prince—she felt her heart racing and her face become flush with shame and embarrassment. It hit her suddenly like a stabbing jolt of reality: He had done everything to prepare for this day. He had done everything to woo her; to bless her, to capture her heart, and now was here to rescue her…and she had done nothing! She had nothing to offer Him. No gifts. No guests. She reflected back on her life and realized she had labored and sweated over all the wrong things and for all the wrong reasons. The depth of her shame was so intense that she grabbed the hem of her gown and turned, ready to run away. It was then that her eyes met His.

There in His eyes she saw something in His gaze that was more intense than her shame, more powerful than her guilt. That "something" was greater than anything she had ever felt before. She turned back toward Him and slowly continued down the aisle. Then it happened. Not all at once, but gradually. As she walked…as she approached her Prince… as she stared into His loving eyes…her shame began to melt away. Now she could see it: The look on His face was one of pure love, the kind of love that says, "You are mine, and nothing you have said or done can keep us apart … My princess." As the bride-to-be stepped up to stand next to her Groom, her Lord, every negative emotion lost its grip on her and departed forever. Every pain that had burrowed its way into her soul disappeared once and for all. As she stood there in His presence… face-to-face He smiled tenderly and gently wiped away the tears from her cheek, embraced His new bride and said… "You will never cry again my love…Welcome Home!"

For your Maker is your husband— the LORD Almighty is his name— the Holy One of Israel is your Redeemer; He is called the God of all the earth.
Isaiah 54:5, NIV

For the time has come for the wedding feast of the Lamb, and His bride has prepared herself. She has been given the finest of pure white linen to wear. For the fine linen represents the good deeds of God's holy people.
Rev 19:7, NLT

GET A LOVE LIFE

*Jesus replied, "Love the Lord your God with all your heart
and with all your soul and with all your mind. This is the first
and greatest commandment."*
Matt. 22:37, NIV

Our Lord knows how hard it is for His princesses to keep their eyes on someone they can't yet see. But it is possible. Remember dreaming about true love? You didn't have a face, but you had a hope in your heart and longed for your prince to one day appear.

Treasure of Truth

**You can hear Him speak to you… in His Word
You can see His power… when you pray
You can enter into His presence… by praising Him
You can feel Him comfort you… when you cry
out to Him**

HIS PRINCESS LOVE LETTER TO YOU

My Princess and My delight,

It brings Me great pleasure to see internal beauty blossom inside of you and to watch you grow up in Me. I delight in every moment we spend together. I delight in giving you the desires of your heart. I delight in hearing you call out to Me. Don't ever feel like you're unimportant to Me. There is no reason for you to feel unsure of My love for you. I am always waiting for you to delight yourself in Me and in My love. It is My pleasure to bless you abundantly. Don't look to anyone else to meet your deepest wants and needs, because you will only end up empty and disappointed. Only I can turn your tears into joy and fill the emptiness in your heart. So delight yourself in Me, and you will live life to the fullest because you are My delight.

Love, Your King and your Lord of Eternal Delight.

Treasure of Truth

Our Prince longs to give us back
our hopes and dreams for the future.
He is waiting to refresh
our souls and love us back to life again.
The greatest thing about falling
in love with your Prince is that...

He will never reject you.
He will never disappoint you.
He will never leave you or forsake you.

The more you allow yourself to love Him,
The more you will feel His Holy and loving presence with you and within you.

HIS PRINCESS PRAYER

Dear Lord,

Deliver me into Your arms of love. I'm ready to fall in love with You-and You alone- with all that I am. Break down the wall I have built around my heart and heal me from the wounds and scars left by those who have hurt me. I need to know You are really with me. Reveal Yourself in a very real way, Jesus. I want to believe I am Yours now and forever throughout eternity.

In Your precious name I pray, amen.

HIS PRINCESS PRAYER FOR YOU

My Sister Princess,

I pray in Jesus name that you'll experience the love of Christ, though it is so great you will never fully understand it. And that you will be will be filled with the fullness of life and power that comes from God. I pray you will know the Prince of Peace so intimately that you would never again doubt that you are loved.

Amen.

> *And may you have the power to understand, as all God's people should, how wide, how long, how high, and how deep his love is. May you experience the love of Christ, though it is too great to understand fully. Then you will be made complete with all the fullness of life and power that comes from God.*
> Ephesians 3:18-19, NLT

GET REAL WITH YOUR PRINCE

I pour out my complaints before him and tell him all my troubles. When I am overwhelmed, you alone know the way I should turn.
Psalm 142:2-3, NLT

*E*ven though we have yet to meet our Prince face-to-face, He knows everything about us. Nothing is hidden from Him. He is waiting to have a very authentic and deep relationship with His bride-to-be.

We have a beautiful example in the Psalms of what a real relationship is like with the Lord. Our beloved King David is called "a man after [God's] own heart" (1 Samuel 13:14, AMP). There was nothing artificial about David's relationship with the Lord. If you read any of his Psalms, you will see that David was extremely honest with his God. He didn't hide his rage, his fears, his disappointments, his worries, his praise or his love from his heavenly Father. If you have not experienced that same closeness with Him, it may be because you have never known how to let yourself be entirely honest with Him. You can and will experience the intimacy you long for if you will take a chance and trade a mechanical religious relationship for a totally transparent and real relationship with the One who gave His life to save you—the One you will be spending all of eternity with.

Earlier we talked about how David overcame the temptation to kill King Saul when he had the chance. What we did not talk about is the very "real" and heartfelt prayer he cried out to God. It's found in Psalm 109:8 and you'll see there that David boldly asked that Saul's days be few and that God would replace him with a different king. This was David's eloquent way of saying, "Please let Saul go away somewhere in the wilderness and die!"

So don't listen when the enemy of your soul suggests that you can save yourself from the pain and problems of this world. When something hurts you or someone angers you, tell your Savior all about it. You don't have to wait for your Lord's return to begin to experience intimacy with Him! He is with you now in spirit, so cry out to Him about whatever is on your heart. Don't waste another moment walking alone. Your Prince is waiting for you to speak to Him, so open your heart and let Him love you and bless you with a peace that surpasses all human understanding.

HIS PRINCESS LOVE LETTER TO YOU

My Princess,

*D*on't be afraid to be your real self with me. I know everything about you already, My love. I know how many hairs are on your head. I know when you lie down and when you are awake. I am your Prince, and I gave up my life so that you might have complete access to the throne room of heaven. It breaks My heart to see you in need and not coming to Me. I can and will meet your every need if you will allow Me into your life. I promise to always be your safe place and your Prince of peace.

So come to Me now in truth. There is nothing you can tell Me that will change the way I feel about you. I love when you come to Me and share your feelings, your failings, and your fears. I can more fully reveal My power to you when you come to Me in complete honesty. I also want you to know how passionately I love you, but I will not ever force your honesty. So I wait patiently until you are ready.

Love,
Your Prince, who is everything you are searching for.

*For I know the one in whom I trust, and I am sure
that he is able to safely guard all that I have given him
until the day of his return.*
2 Timothy 1:12, TLB

Write a very "Real" prayer to your King. Tell Him
whatever is really inside your soul and get ready to
feel His Spirit hold you as a daddy holds his little
girl when she cries.

_____

_____

_____

_____

_____

_____

_____

_____

_____

_____

_____

_____

_____

_____

GET OVER YOURSELF

For the LORD is your security.
He will keep your foot from being caught in a trap.
Proverbs 3:26 NLT

Though an army besiege me, My heart will not fear,
Though war break out against me, even then will I be confident
Psalm 27:3, NIV

**There is a big difference between who
we think we are and who our King says
we are according to His written word.**

We all have inadequacies and insecurities...

- Moses was speech-impaired yet was the one chosen to set God's people free from their Egyptian enemies.

- David was a shepherd boy with a father who did not believe in him.

- Gideon was a scaredy cat who was bound by fear until the Lord addressed him as a valiant warrior.

• Mary was just a teenager who no one believed
was a young virgin before Christ was born.

• Sarah was childless and probably in menopause
when our God promised she would have
offspring as numerous as the stars.

The only way we will ever get over ourselves is to
make a choice to trade our Self-Confidence for God
Confidence.

TREASURE OF TRUTH

You are...
Chosen by God...

*But you are a chosen people, a royal priesthood, a holy nation,
a people belonging to God, that you may declare the praises of
him who called you out of darkness into his wonderful light.*
1 Peter 2:9, NIV

A new creation...

*This means that anyone who belongs to Christ has become a
new person. The old life is gone; a new life has begun!*
2 Corinthians 5:17, NLT

Light to this Dark world...

*Yes, I am sending you to the Gentiles to open their eyes, so
they may turn from darkness to light and from the power of
Satan to God. Then they will receive forgiveness for their sins
and be given a place among God's people, who are set apart
by faith in me.*
Acts 26:17-18, NLT

Holy and Pure in His sight...

*For he chose us in him before the creation of the world to be
holy and blameless in his sight.*
Ephesians 1:4, NIV

Crowned in Victory...

*For the LORD your God is going with you! He will fight for
you against your enemies, and he will give you victory!'*
Deuteronomy 20:4, NLT

A Trophy of His Grace...

*For it is by grace you have been saved, through faith—
and this not from yourselves, it is the gift of God.*
Ephesians 2:8, NIV

His Princess Warrior...

*I have fought the good fight, I have finished the race,
I have kept the faith.*
2 Timothy 4:7, NIV

His Bride to be...

*Let us rejoice and be glad and give him glory!
For the wedding of the Lamb has come,
and his bride has made herself ready.*
Revelation 19:7, NIV

HIS PRINCESS PRAYER

Dear Jesus,

*P*lease help me remember that I am a part of Your forever kingdom and Your eternal plan. Open my eyes to Your majesty and love so that I will see myself as royalty. Do not let me waste another day not living for You and not loving You with all my heart. I give You all that I am. Align my dreams and goals with Your perfect plan for me. Help me let go of anything that is keeping me from obeying You and knowing Your blessings. I love You, Lord, and I want to show You my love with my life. I choose on this day to take my royal position as Your light to the world.

In Jesus' name I pray, amen.

HIS PRINCESS IN ACTION

What do you personally struggle with getting over?
Confess it in a prayer right now.

_____
_____
_____
_____
_____
_____
_____
_____
_____
_____
_____
_____
_____
_____
_____
_____
_____
_____
_____
_____

HIS PRINCESS LOVE LETTER TO YOU

My Princess,

You are my masterpiece. I love what I have created. I am delighted in you! Don't ever feel insecure about what you think you are not, because I made you in My image and your uniqueness is a gift from Me. I did not give you a life, My love, for you to squeeze into a man-made mold. You are royalty, but you won't discover that truth by gazing into a mirror. Let Me be your mirror and I will reflect back to you your true beauty. The more you gaze at Me, the more you will see My workmanship in you. The sooner you see yourself for who you really are, the sooner you can begin your reign as My priceless Princess with a purpose.

Love,
Your King and your Creator.

For we are God's [own] handiwork (His workmanship), recreated in Christ Jesus, [born anew] that we may do those good works which God predestined (planned beforehand) for us [taking paths which He prepared ahead of time], that we should walk in them [living the good life which He prearranged and made ready for us to live].
Ephesians 2:10, AMP

Get Faith

Jesus said, "I tell you the truth, anyone who has faith in me will do what I have been doing. He will do even greater things than these, because I am going to the Father."
John 14:12, NIV

HIS PRINCESS DEVOTION

What is Faith?

Faith is the confidence that what we hope for will actually happen; it gives us assurance about things we cannot see.
Hebrews 11:1, NLT

He longs for us to truly trust Him and to take Him at His Word. Many times our faith in Him grows during life's most difficult and challenging circumstances. For instance, can you imagine what kind of faith it must have taken Mary, the mother of Jesus? Think about it… imagine a sixteen-year-old virgin being told by an angel that she was pregnant by the Holy Spirit and that she would deliver the Son of God, the Savior of the world! What would her fiancé think—and do? But she trusted God and His plan for her life.

And then there's Noah. Today his story is famous because of the faith he had. But when he was building an ark, there was not a sign of rain in the sky. I'm sure that his neighbors mocked him, and his wife, sons, and daughters-in-law- certainly asked him many times, "Are you sure God is really going to flood the earth?" Yet Noah's family followed his leadership because of their faith in God, and we all know how the story ends.

Remember Sarah? When God first promised her a baby, she had faith, but over time she got tired of waiting on the Lord and His timing. So she decided to help God's promise be fulfilled and had her husband sleep with a servant so she could have the baby she longed for. As her plan unfolded, though, Sarah found herself jealous, bitter, and miserable. But our gracious God still gave her Isaac, the baby son He had promised. What an awesome promise from our Prince!

Read this scripture out loud.

No one will be able to stand against you all the days of your life. As I was with Moses so I will be with you. I will never leave you nor forsake you
Joshua 1:5, NIV

HIS PRINCESS IN ACTION

I don't know about you, but I've sure felt like the disciples must have felt as they clung to their boat out on the stormy seas. When storms have hit my life, I've wondered—as I'm guessing those disciples did—Is my Lord sleeping while I'm drowning in my troubles and my worries? Is He going to rescue me from this fear, or will it overtake me? But then I think about Jesus asking Peter to walk out on the water. Peter didn't begin to sink until he took his eyes off his Lord and focused on his circumstances, some what-ifs, and the very real possibility that he could drown (Matthew 14:30). The disciples—especially Peter—teach us the secret to true faith…and that is to keep our eyes locked on our Lord, not on our lives.

Here are some of the things we can do to keep our eyes steadily on our Prince:

> 1. We can turn fear into faith by choosing to pray instead of worry.
>
> 2. We can go immediately to His Word and remind ourselves of who He is and review His promises.

3. We can play praise music throughout our day to stay focused on Him.

4. We can call a friend to pray for us, especially when we feel too weak to pray for ourselves.

5. We can write down a specific promise from His Word regarding our situation and either memorize it or post it where we will see it often.

6. We can write prayers (our love letters to God) in a journal. This is a physical act by which we hand the situation over to our Lord. And in the future, when we face new challenges, we will be able to look back and read about His faithfulness to us in the past.

Notes: _____
_____
_____
_____
_____
_____

GET A PRAYER LIFE WITH PURPOSE

You can ask for anything in my name, and I will do it, so that the Son can bring glory to the Father. Yes, ask me for anything in my name, and I will do it!
John 14:13-14, NLT

HIS PRINCESS DEVOTION

Pray in the Spirit at all times and on every occasion. Stay alert and be persistent in your prayers for all believers everywhere.
Ephesians 6:18, NLT

I know from personal experience how hard it can be to believe that the God of the entire universe hears our prayers. I also used to think that there must be some magic formula I needed in order to make God's hand move when I asked. But today I know that we who name Jesus "Savior" really are royalty, that God really does hear our prayers, and that we have "anytime" access to the throne room of our King. When we begin to pray about everything, and especially when we pray with purpose, supernatural things happen. When we ask for God to do great things to further His kingdom, He always makes something great happen.

We need Prayer to have.....

- Compassion for others.
- Courage to stand up for righteousness.
- Conviction to live for Christ.
- Character that reflects we are God's.
- Commitment to God's call on our lives.

John Wesley says...

"Get on fire for God and people will come watch you burn."

HIS PRINCESS PRAYER

Dear God,

I want to pray with purpose. Help me to know that You hear me when I call to You—and give me the courage to ask You to do great things. Remind me that it is my privilege to come to you in all things—and thank You that You care enough to listen to my every request.

In Jesus' name I pray, amen.

HIS PRINCESS DEVOTION

The enemy doesn't have to completely defeat us in order to win the battle for our energy and time. All he has to do is distract us, and his victory comes easily. And we know distraction, don't we? Nothing burns us women out more than excessive busyness. No time to rest, relax, reflect, or restore ourselves. Somehow we feel—consciously or otherwise—that if our schedules aren't packed with places to go, people to see, and endless things to do, we must not be important. Or maybe we are so concerned about what others will think that we are not willing to set healthy boundaries. When my schedule gets overloaded, my family suffers, my health suffers, and my relationship with God suffers. The devil wants us weak on all these fronts because then he can take us down.

Keep in mind that "if the devil can't make us bad, his next trick is to make us busy." If we are too busy to spend time with God or too busy to spend time with the loved ones who need us, than we are busier than our King wants us to be. We need to set our schedule so that it accurately reflects our priorities. To help you determine those priorities, ask yourself the following questions:

- What really matters most to me in my life?

- In what ways can I be replaced—and in what roles am I genuinely irreplaceable?

- Am I overwhelmed by my schedule?

- Is my health suffering because I have no time to rest?

- Am I spending enough time with those people I love?

- When I say yes to something, to what am I saying no?

- Do I set healthy boundaries around my schedule and commitments?

When we don't make time for our Prince or for those He has entrusted to our care, we break His heart. And keep in mind that if you don't have time for your kids when they are young, they won't have time for you when you are old. The way we spend our time teaches our children how to spend their time when they are grown.

HIS PRINCESS LOVE LETTER TO YOU

My Princess,

Give Me your plans. I know you have ideas in your mind about how everything should unfold in your life. You even have an agenda for this very day. But because I love you, I need you to give Me back all your plans for today—and for all your tomorrows. Remember, My love, that My ways are not your ways. If you will give Me a chance, I will show you how I want you to spend your days. I've ordained different seasons of life for different purposes. I know your heart longs to do many things. But if you will be available to Me, I will do more for you than you could ever do for yourself.

Love,
Your King who is always available to you.

The Lord directs the steps of the godly.
He delights in every detail of their lives.
Psalm 37:23, NLT

His Princess™ Retreat

WORKBOOK

HIS PRINCESS IN ACTION

Ask yourself the following questions:

What are the top five things that really matter most to me in my life?

1. _____
2. _____
3. _____
4. _____
5. _____

Does my schedule reflect my top five priorities?
Yes___ No_____

What needs most of my attention during this season of my life?

1. _____
2. _____
3. _____

Make it happen! By applying your answers below to your life.

In what ways can I be replaced?

1. _____
2. _____
3. _____

In what roles am I genuinely irreplaceable?

1. _____
2 _____
3. _____

What thing(s) are proving more than I can handle in my schedule right now?

1. _____
2. _____
3. _____
4. _____

What can I cut from my schedule that will give me a more balanced and healthy life?

_____

_____

Do I set healthy boundaries around my schedule
and commitments? *(Write out your ideal schedule that
allows time for relationships and refreshment to your soul).*

Morning _____

_____

Mid Morning _____

_____

Noon time _____

_____

Afternoon_____

_____

Dinner time _____

_____

Evening_____

_____

Ideal bedtime _____

_____

Weekends _____

_____

HIS PRINCESS PRAYER

Dear Lord,

*P*lease take control of my schedule—and convict me, Holy Spirit, about what's on my calendar that is not of kingdom or eternal value. I want to invest wisely my days on this earth. Help me to spend more time with You so I can hear Your voice despite life's busyness. Forgive me, God, for being too busy for what really matters—for living out my love for You and my love for others. I surrender my schedule to You.

Amen.

Treasure of Truth
If the Devil can't make us Bad
His next trick... is to make us Busy

Get an Eternal View
So we don't look at the troubles we can see now; rather, we fix our gaze on things that cannot be seen. For the things we see now will soon be gone, but the things we cannot see will last forever.
2 Corinthians 4:18, NLT

Our Prince will rescue us from the troubles of this world, but the fact is that this life can hit extremely hard at times. At those times the hope of heaven is the only thing we have to hold on to, and even though it may not feel like it, that is all we need. We will be able to make our mark for all eternity while we are here when we focus on the hope of the good things to come once we are finally home in His loving arms.

HIS PRINCESS DEVOTION

We will never truly know that our God is all we need until He is all we have to hold on to.

We have all had times in our lives when we wonder how we will get through to the other side of the circumstances or the pain. Even our Prince cried out to His Father in heaven and said, "Father, why have you forsaken me?" (Matthew 27:46). But He kept His eyes on His Father and on His Father's eternal purpose. If our Savior hadn't kept His eyes fixed on eternity, we would never get our "happily ever after." Thank You, Jesus! His death on the cross gives us hope for the future as well as hope for the present.

Now, I've been in ministry for several years, and many people's stories have made me wonder where God was in their pain and how they could have found any hope in the darkness. One particular story is engraved in my memory. I received a phone call from a nurse who was taking care of an AIDS patient named Cindy. The nurse said Cindy had been reading one of my books and wanted to talk to me about God before she died. Being passionate about any opportunity to lead someone to the Lord, I said, "Of course I'll call Cindy!"

But the nurse put something of a damper on my enthusiasm when she described in an email the situation I was walking into. I won't go into detail about Cindy's life, but I will say that it was the worst story of abuse by men I have ever heard, and now she was going to die because of their sin. I found myself feeling very afraid to call Cindy. I told the Lord that I could not tell her He was a good God, and I felt paralyzed and unable to pray after hearing her excruciatingly painful story. So I asked others to pray for me.

After five days of fighting with God in my spirit, and urgent messages and pleas from Cindy's nurse,

I finally picked up the phone and dialed the hospital where she was. Cindy answered, and God gave me these words of eternal truth:

Cindy, I know that men have done horrible things to you, and I know that many of them called themselves Christians, but, they weren't acting like God's people! I beg you not to let those men keep you from going to a place where your heavenly Father will wipe away every tear you have ever cried. Ask Jesus into your heart and forgive those men, and I promise that you will be in a place where no one will ever hurt you again. You will be in the arms of the very God who died for you and who longs to spend eternity with you.

Cindy hung up on me, and I was devastated—until one week later when her nurse called me. She told me that Cindy had asked Jesus into her heart and had asked the nurse to tell me that she will see me in heaven.

- It was an eternal view that gave me the courage to call Cindy and tell her about heaven.

• It was an eternal view that gave Cindy the will to forgive those men and let her new found Prince take her home.

We live in a fallen world, and tragically, innocent people suffer because of the sins of others. Pain is an inevitable part of this life, but as the King's chosen bride, we are not to take our eyes off eternity. We who are His chosen ones are the only ones who can share with this world the good news about Jesus and eternal life; the good news of the hope that we have in our King.

Our Prince is preparing our home in heaven, and no eye has seen, no ear has heard, and no mind has imagined the things He has prepared for those who love Him (1 Corinthians 2:9). We are definitely not home yet! And we all have people around us who need the Savior. So let us fight the good fight as Paul did, and complete our royal call as Queen Esther did, until it is time for our Lord to rescue us.

Treasure of Truth
Remember this truth: If we never receive one worldly blessing while we are here, we still have all we need and more because:

We have eternal life.
We have eternal hope.
We have peace of mind and spirit.
We have God's power inside of us.
We have a home waiting for us in Heaven.
We have a real Prince who is coming soon.
We will live happily ever after when this life is over.
We do not know the time or date of our wedding with the Prince. But we do know He is coming, and He wants us to be ready for His return.

HIS PRINCESS LEGACY

The way we live today is the legacy we will be leaving behind us.

ASK YOURSELF...

- What will I be remembered for when I am gone?
- What have I contributed to the lives of those I love?
- For what do I want to be remembered?

I saw the Holy City, the new Jerusalem, coming down out of heaven from God, prepared as a bride beautifully dressed for her husband. And I heard a loud voice from the throne saying, "Now the dwelling of God is with men, and he will live with them. They will be his people, and God himself will be with them and be their God. He will wipe every tear from their eyes. There will be no more death or mourning or crying or pain, for the old order of things has passed away." He who was seated on the throne said, "I am making everything new!" Then he said, "Write this down, for these words are trustworthy and true."
Revelation 21:2-5, NIV

"I am the Alpha and the Omega, the Beginning and the End."
Revelation 21:6, NIV

FINAL GROUP DISCUSSION

Take turns reading once again these Treasures of Truth:

His Princess Beauty

A Beautiful Heart...
That Is Full of His Love and Free to Love Others

*So that Christ may dwell in your hearts through faith; and
that you, being rooted and grounded in love, may be able to
comprehend with all the saints what is the breadth and length
and height and depth, and to know the love of Christ which
surpasses knowledge, that you may be filled up to all the
fullness of God.*
Ephesians 3:17–19, NASB

A Beautiful Mind...
That Is Focused on Your Purpose

*But the plans of the LORD stand firm forever, the purposes
of his heart through all generations.*
Psalm 33:11, NIV

Beautiful Lips...
That Speak Words of Wisdom, Encouragement, and Life!

The Sovereign LORD has given me his words of wisdom, so that I know what to say to all these weary ones. Morning by morning he wakens me and opens my understanding to his will.
Isaiah 50:4, NLT

Beautiful Feet...
That Walk in God Confidence and Lead Others to Him

How beautiful upon the mountains are the feet of him who brings good news, who proclaims peace, who brings glad tidings of good things, who proclaims salvation, who says to Zion, "Your God reigns!"
Isaiah 52:7, NKJV

Beautiful Hands...
That Reach Out to Those Who Are in Need

She opens her hand to the poor, yes, she reaches out her filled hands to the needy [whether in body, mind, or spirit].
Proverbs 31:20, AMP

Beautiful Eyes...
That See with an Eternal Perspective

So we don't look at the troubles we can see now; rather, we fix our gaze on things that cannot be seen. For the things we see now will soon be gone, but the things we cannot see will last forever.
2 Corinthians 4:18, NLT

A Beautiful Life ...
That Will Forever Be Remembered

Praise the LORD! How joyful are those who fear the LORD and delight in obeying his commands. Their children will be successful everywhere; an entire generation of godly people will be blessed. They themselves will be wealthy, and their good deeds will last forever.
Psalm 112:1–3, NLT

Notes: _____

_____

_____

_____

_____

_____

_____

_____

_____

_____

_____

_____

_____

_____

_____

_____

_____

_____

HIS PRINCESS LOVE LETTER TO YOU

My Princess...

YOU BEGIN AND END WITH ME

*Y*ou need not worry when your life will end, My precious child. All you need to know is that your first breath began with Me, and your last breath will lead you to My presence. Don't ever let fear of death or eternity frighten you. Your todays and tomorrows are secure with Me—I have held them in My hand since the beginning of time. When you finish your brief time on earth and I call you into My presence, your forever life in heaven will begin. But for now, My chosen one, you must live free from fear. Instead, trust Me to take you through every trial that comes your way. Remember that nothing in the universe can separate us. I am with you always...even until the end of time. So live well and finish strong—fixing your hope on the day that we will meet face-to-face on the other side of eternity.

Love,
Your Eternal King.

It is...
Our Character... Not our Appearance
Our Choices... Not our Possessions
Our Courage... Not our Comfort
Our Compassion... Not our Successes

These are the jewels that people will truly treasure when we're gone.

My Prayer for you as we close our time together is this:

My dear princess,

May you never again doubt how much you are loved by your Prince and how important you are in our King's eternal plan. I also pray that our Prince will put a passion in your soul so intense that you will have the courage to take your royal position and possess a deep conviction to live boldly as the princess you are destined to be.

In Jesus' name I lift you up and pray, amen.

A note from Sheri Rose:

Thank you for the Honor of Sharing my Heart with You. My Prayer is that you Experience the Love of God in such a way that you will Never Forget Who You Really Are... "His Princess"...A Treasured Daughter of the King. Always remember to walk through this Life in God-confidence and Great Faith in your Father in Heaven. You will Leave a Legacy that will Impact all Those who Watched you Love and Follow Your Lord.

I would love to stay connected with you. Please visit my website and sign up for my newsletter and ministry updates.

 Your Sister Princess,
Sheri Rose

*To order any of the products
listed on the following pages
please visit our website:*

www.hisprincess.com
or 602-407-8789

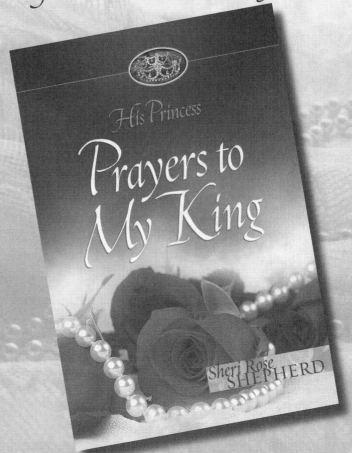

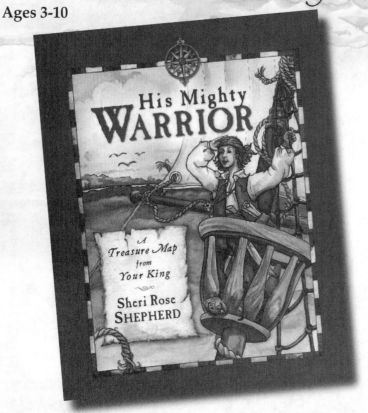

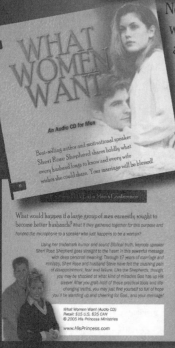